D1718892

TRAINING
TEACHER
LEADERS

in a PLC at Work®

A GUIDE TO CULTIVATING
SHARED LEADERSHIP

JASMINE K. KULLAR

Solution Tree | Press
a division of
Solution Tree

Copyright © 2024 by Solution Tree Press

Materials appearing here are copyrighted. With one exception, all rights are reserved. Readers may reproduce only those pages marked "Reproducible." Otherwise, no part of this book may be reproduced or transmitted in any form or by any means (electronic, photocopying, recording, or otherwise) without prior written permission of the publisher.

555 North Morton Street
Bloomington, IN 47404
800.733.6786 (toll free) / 812.336.7700
FAX: 812.336.7790

email: info@SolutionTree.com
SolutionTree.com

Visit **go.SolutionTree.com/PLCbooks** to download the free reproducibles in this book.

Printed in the United States of America

Library of Congress Cataloging-in-Publication Data

Names: Kullar, Jasmine K., 1976- author.
Title: Training teacher leaders in a PLC at work : a guide to cultivating
   shared leadership / Jasmine K. Kullar.
Description: Bloomington, IN : Solution Tree Press, 2024. | Includes
   bibliographical references and index.
Identifiers: LCCN 2024003805 (print) | LCCN 2024003806 (ebook) | ISBN
   9781960574800 (paperback) | ISBN 9781960574817 (ebook)
Subjects: LCSH: Professional learning communities. | Educational
   leadership. | Teachers--Professional relationships.
Classification: LCC LB1731 .K83 2024 (print) | LCC LB1731 (ebook) | DDC
   371.1--dc23/eng/20240226
LC record available at https://lccn.loc.gov/2024003805
LC ebook record available at https://lccn.loc.gov/2024003806

Solution Tree
Jeffrey C. Jones, CEO
Edmund M. Ackerman, President

Solution Tree Press
President and Publisher: Douglas M. Rife
Associate Publishers: Todd Brakke and Kendra Slayton
Editorial Director: Laurel Hecker
Art Director: Rian Anderson
Copy Chief: Jessi Finn
Production Editor: Paige Duke
Copy Editor: Evie Madsen
Proofreader: Jessi Finn
Text and Cover Designer: Fabiana Cochran
Acquisitions Editors: Carol Collins and Hilary Goff
Content Development Specialist: Amy Rubenstein
Associate Editors: Sarah Ludwig and Elijah Oates
Editorial Assistant: Anne Marie Watkins

■ ACKNOWLEDGMENTS

I can't say thank you enough to my amazing family for being my biggest champions! I could not do what I do if it weren't for your encouragement and support. Thanks to Sabrina, my motivator, who would make me sit down to write while she did her homework. Thanks to Dillon, my other motivator, who would wait to watch movies with me until I finished my writing goals for the weekend. And, of course, thanks to my husband, who has always celebrated my work no matter what. Lastly, thanks to my parents and my brother for always pushing me and always being in my corner.

I would like to express my sincere gratitude to so many at Solution Tree, starting with my mentor and dear friend, Claudia Wheatley. Thanks also to Paige Duke, Todd Brakke, Kendra Slayton, and Laurel Hecker from the publishing team for your thoughtful suggestions every step of the way. Thank you to Rian Anderson and Fabiana Cochran for your hard work with the cover design. Thank you to Shik Love and Jamila Loving for your support with marketing. Douglas Rife and Jeff Jones, thank you for your incredible leadership at Solution Tree. I am so grateful for the rewarding opportunities, lifelong friendships, and unique experiences you have provided me during my time with Solution Tree. Thanks also to all the PLC authors and associates who inspire me every day!

Finally, I would not be the educator I am today if it weren't for Richard and Rebecca DuFour. I am forever grateful for the impact they had on me professionally and personally.

Solution Tree Press would like to thank the following reviewers:

John D. Ewald
Education Consultant
Frederick, Maryland

Colleen Fleming
Literacy Specialist
Calgary, Alberta, Canada

Kristen Gibson
Instructional Specialist
Pasadena Independent School District
Pasadena, Texas

Johanna Josaphat
Teacher Leader
Urban Assembly Unison School
Brooklyn, New York

Jed Kees
Principal
Onalaska Middle School
Onalaska, Wisconsin

John Unger
Principal
West Fork Middle School
West Fork, Arkansas

Visit **go.SolutionTree.com/PLCbooks** to
download the free reproducibles in this book.

■ TABLE OF CONTENTS

Reproducibles are in italics.

ABOUT THE AUTHOR

 **Jasmine K. Kullar, EdD,** is a chief school leadership officer overseeing more than one hundred schools in a large metropolitan school district in Georgia. She is also a faculty member in the College of Professional Studies, Educational Leadership Department at a postsecondary institution outside Atlanta, where she has been involved with the national University Principal Preparation Initiative (UPPI) in redesigning university educational leadership programs.

Prior to these roles, Dr. Kullar was an assistant superintendent for five years and a middle school principal for seven years at two separate schools. With many years of school leadership experience, Dr. Kullar has worked at the elementary, middle, and high school levels in North America, giving her a depth of experience. Her journey with professional learning communities (PLCs) began in her first year of teaching, more than two decades ago, when she attended a PLC workshop and heard Richard DuFour and Robert Eaker. Since then, Dr. Kullar has been implementing PLC tenets as a teacher. When she became a school administrator, she led her school to become the first school in the state of Georgia to receive Model PLC at Work® status (see www.allthingsplc.info) and garnered statewide attention for PLCs.

Dr. Kullar has worked with schools and districts in over twenty-five U.S. states. Her work includes speaking at events, facilitating professional development for small and large audiences, coaching teams, and working to develop school and district leadership teams. Her areas of expertise include PLCs, response to intervention, educator wellness, women in leadership, building teacher leadership teams, and supporting teacher teams and leadership.

Dr. Kullar is the author of *Connecting Through Leadership: The Promise of Precise and Effective Communication in Schools*; coauthor of *Building Your Building: How to Hire and Keep Great Teachers* and *The Educator Wellness Plan Book and Journal: Continuous Growth for Each Season of Your Professional Life*; and coeditor of *Women Who Lead: Insights, Inspiration, and Guidance to Grow as an Educator*.

Dr. Kullar earned an undergraduate degree from the University of Toronto, a graduate degree from Memorial University of Newfoundland, and a doctorate from Argosy University in Atlanta. After earning a doctorate, Dr. Kullar continued to learn by participating in various programs and earning several certificates, including from Harvard's Leading Education Systems at the National Level program.

To book Jasmine K. Kullar for professional development, contact pd@SolutionTree.com.

■ INTRODUCTION

School leaders carry incredible responsibility; their influence can make or break a school. As a result, principals in today's schools can no longer lead in isolation—they must involve their teacher leaders. Simply put, leadership must be a collective endeavor.

I learned this during my early years of principalship. To truly make an impact on student achievement, I had to implement a professional learning community (PLC). I couldn't do it without more leaders in my school, so I began building a shared understanding on my campus of what it means to be a PLC and what that work entails. The teacher leaders I selected to help me lead this work were excited and devoted to the initiative. I was elated! However, that excitement and commitment didn't extend beyond those teacher leaders. Their biggest challenge was influencing their teacher teams to embrace the PLC process. In short, leading their colleagues was the hard part.

I switched gears and started focusing on developing teacher leaders' *ability to lead*. To earn my school leadership certification, I attended leadership classes, workshops, and conferences and read many leadership articles. This was essential information my teacher leaders hadn't encountered in their professional lives.

I wrote this book to similarly help school leaders provide teacher leaders the skills they need to successfully lead others on their campus. Use this as a resource with your school leadership teams (composed of school administrators and teacher leaders) to help team members become strong leaders so together you can impact student achievement.

Why PLC

Teacher leaders historically help school administrators lead. Oftentimes, when school or district leaders want their school to become a PLC, administrators turn to teacher leaders to help with that journey. Shared leadership is a critical component to the PLC process.

While shared leadership is useful in all schools, it's essential in PLCs. Educators and coauthors Kenneth C. Williams and Tom Hierck (2015) explain why:

> A school's transition to a PLC requires leadership at all levels. A school leader can bring a topic to the forefront, frame a discussion, facilitate healthy, productive conflict, and provide the resources and support to move forward with the initiative. But school leaders alone cannot effect the sustained cultural change required to become a PLC. (p. 17)

Let's begin by defining terms. What exactly is *a PLC*? When educational researchers Richard DuFour and Robert Eaker wrote *Professional Learning Communities at Work* in 1998, they thought deeply about what the words they selected meant (as cited in DuFour, DuFour, Eaker, Mattos, & Muhammad, 2021).

A *professional* is someone who has expertise in a specific area. Professionals have completed advanced training in the field and also remain current as things evolve.

Learning refers to the shift from focusing on teaching to focusing on learning—instead of what teachers *taught*, we measure what students *learned*. *Learning* also refers to educators participating in an ongoing process of continual growth as lifelong learners. In PLCs, educators are expected to continually study and learn to better themselves as educators.

Finally, *community* refers to educators collaborating, which allows them to learn from one another and take collective responsibility for student success.

Putting these terms together defines a *professional learning community* as:

> An ongoing process in which educators work collaboratively in recurring cycles of collective inquiry and action research to achieve better results for the students they serve. PLCs operate under the assumption that the key to improved learning for students is continuous, job-embedded learning for educators. (DuFour, DuFour, Eaker, Many, Mattos, & Muhammad, 2024, p. 14)

There are three big ideas that drive the PLC process: (1) focus on learning, (2) collaborative culture and collective responsibility, and (3) a results orientation (DuFour et al., 2024).

1. **Focus on learning:** In a PLC, school leaders ensure all students learn at high levels. As teams collaborate, they focus on the four critical questions (DuFour & Fullan, 2013):

    1. What is it we want our students to learn? What knowledge, skills, and dispositions do we expect them to acquire as a result of this course, this grade level, and this unit of instruction?
    2. How will we know if each student is learning each of the skills, concepts, and dispositions we have deemed most essential?
    3. How will we respond when some of our students do not learn? What process will we put in place to ensure students receive additional time and support for learning in a way that is timely, precise, diagnostic, directive, and systematic?
    4. How will we enrich and extend the learning for students who are already proficient? (p. 15)

    In addition to having a focus on learning, school leaders examine all practices, policies, and procedures to ensure they are advancing student learning. Too often, school practices, policies, and procedures are rooted in maintaining the status quo or keeping the adults happy. A *focus on learning* means school leaders base all decisions on what is best for student learning; learning drives everything. "Every potential organizational practice, policy, and procedure is assessed on the basis of this question: Will this ensure higher levels of learning for our students?" (DuFour et al., 2024, p. 18).

2. **Collaborative culture and collective responsibility:** Collaboration is not optional in a PLC. Teachers are organized into teams and they work "*interdependently* to achieve *common goals* for which members are *mutually accountable*" (DuFour et al., 2024, p. 57). When teachers collaborate, students benefit from the expertise of all the teachers, instead of just one. Teachers collaborate to learn from one another and become better teachers for their students as a result.

3. **Results orientation:** Assessing all the collaboration and work teachers do is based on results, not intentions. It's not necessarily about the hard work, time, and effort teachers put into the work; it's about the *results*. What impact does all that have on student learning? There must be a systematic way for teachers to review student results frequently and then to act on those results.

It's impactful when teacher leaders learn about the three big ideas and four critical questions to help lead the work because this knowledge equips teachers to thrive in a PLC culture. However, none of that guarantees teachers will be effective *teacher leaders*. Teachers know how to lead their students, but leading adults requires a different skill set, especially when those adults are colleagues. This lack of leadership training for teacher leaders is a common challenge in successfully implementing PLCs. Teachers may have the knowledge to lead a PLC, but they frequently lack the leadership skills they need to influence their colleagues. Teacher leaders need those leadership skills to work alongside the principal, but they also need those leadership skills to continue to lead the PLC work even after principal leaves.

In *Cultures Built to Last: Systemic PLCs at Work*, coauthors Richard DuFour and Michael Fullan (2013) write about the need for many leaders for widespread leadership in a PLC:

> Implementing significant change requires shared leadership and a collective effort. Widespread leadership is equally imperative for sustaining that improvement effort. Leaders don't emerge from a vacuum, however, so effective systemic reform requires ensuring the next generation of leaders is available to carry the reform further. This means today's leaders must take deliberate steps to nurture the development of people throughout the organization to serve as tomorrow's leaders. (p. 71)

This book aims to help school leaders take those deliberate steps to develop leadership skills in their teacher leaders.

The Ten Key Leadership Skills

Many teacher leaders hesitate to embody strong leadership skills because they don't have a title and feel they have no authority to tell their colleagues what to do. But great leadership isn't about having authority over your colleagues. Karyn Gordon (2021), CEO of DK Leadership, a global leadership coaching company, explains it this way:

> Great leadership is simply a set of skills that are first learned internally, which means all of us can develop it. Great leadership is not about having a title. In fact, a title or supervisory role is simply an external opportunity for a person to exercise and strengthen their leadership skills. A job is not going to suddenly bestow leadership abilities on you—you have to acquire them on your own. (p. 1)

The antidote to teacher leader reticence isn't a title but proper training in developing the skills they need to effectively lead their colleagues. School leaders can do this by taking the time to train teacher leaders on leadership and helping them develop the following ten leadership skills.

1. Self-confidence
2. Courage
3. Conflict resolution
4. Lifelong learning
5. Emotional intelligence
6. Change leadership
7. Innovation
8. Decision making
9. Problem solving
10. Communication

Figure I.1 illustrates these ten key leadership skills. Notice that skills 1–5 have an internal focus, whereas skills 6–10 have an external focus.

FIGURE I.1: Profile of a PLC teacher leader.

By intentionally working on strengthening each of these important leadership skills, teacher leaders ultimately strengthen their overall ability to lead others. There is no question school leaders must provide the support and professional development to train teacher leaders; principals need the help of teacher leaders to accomplish the work of a PLC. Educators and coauthors Richard DuFour and Rebecca DuFour (2012) write: "Those who study the leadership of both schools and organizations in general would offer very consistent advice to principals: no single person has all of the energy and expertise to effectively address all of the responsibilities of leadership" (p. 8). All school principals and district leaders must make the investment to help grow and cultivate leadership capabilities in teacher leaders. This book is designed to help school leadership teams do that in collaboration.

About This Book

This book is divided into two parts. Part 1 explores foundational concepts, such as why teacher leaders are needed in a PLC, barriers to successful teacher leadership, and processes for selecting teacher leaders.

- » Chapter 1 discusses how changes to the principal's role make shared leadership essential for the success of a PLC.
- » Chapter 2 explores common barriers to teacher leadership and ways to overcome them.
- » Chapter 3 shares methods principals can use to select teacher leaders.

Part 2 takes a close look at the ten leadership skills, devoting one chapter to each skill. Each chapter in part 2 provides information about that leadership skill, articulates the skill's connection to PLCs, and offers professional development activities for developing the skill.

- » Chapter 4 discusses developing self-confidence skills.
- » Chapter 5 discusses developing courage.
- » Chapter 6 discusses developing conflict-resolution skills.
- » Chapter 7 discusses developing lifelong-learning skills.
- » Chapter 8 discusses developing emotional intelligence.
- » Chapter 9 discusses developing change-leadership skills.
- » Chapter 10 discusses developing innovation skills.
- » Chapter 11 discusses developing decision-making skills.

» Chapter 12 discusses developing problem-solving skills.

» Chapter 13 discusses developing communication skills.

The part 2 chapters each have activities, reflections, and next steps school leadership teams can use to develop and strengthen teacher leaders' leadership skills.

This book guides school leaders to build and develop teacher leaders. Author, speaker, and consultant Michael Fullan (2014) writes, "The principal's role is to lead the school's teachers in a process of learning to improve their teaching, while learning alongside them about what works and what doesn't" (p. 55). Use this book to learn about leadership skills together and understand what is working and what is not working. Are you ready? Let's get started!

PART 1

Part 1 is designed to help school leaders set the stage for building school leadership teams by exploring the *why*, *what*, and *how*.

Why are teacher leaders so important in schools? The idea of teacher leaders isn't new. However, to maximize their role, principals must thoroughly understand why they need shared leadership in the first place, and why teacher leaders are essential to the work of a PLC.

What barriers do teacher leaders face to successful leadership? Without addressing barriers, principals struggle to build an effective school leadership team.

Finally, how do school leaders select teacher leaders? Designing a robust process for selecting teacher leaders can help establish shared leadership from the beginning.

CHAPTER 1

Why Principals Need Teacher Leaders

Principals cannot be the lone leaders in schools. Researchers Daniel Goleman, Richard Boyatzis, and Annie McKee (2013) write: "There are many leaders, not just one. Leadership is distributed. It resides not solely in the individual at the top, but in every person at every level who, in one way or another, acts as a leader to a group of followers" (p. xviii). Principals must embrace shared leadership to effectively implement professional learning communities, which ultimately improve student achievement.

For shared leadership to be effective, principals must recognize that teacher leaders have *followers*—fellow teachers the teacher leaders are responsible for leading in their department or grade level. Teacher leaders are rarely prepared to lead their colleagues because they may not have the specific leadership skill set they need to assert influence. Principals must develop teacher leaders' leadership skills. For that time investment, principals gain more leaders at every level of the school, all working together to lead the PLC process.

In this chapter, I explore the challenges principals face due to changes in their role. Fortunately, shared leadership provides a solution to these challenges. After discussing the benefits of sharing leadership with teachers, I take a closer look at teacher leadership in a PLC. Finally, I examine ten skills of successful teacher leaders.

Challenges of the Principal's Role

There is no question the job of the principal has changed since the 1980s. Traditionally, principals functioned primarily as operational leaders. They managed people, ensured teachers had the appropriate textbooks and resources they needed, administered discipline to students when needed, and ensured the overall physical maintenance of the school building. However, today's principals are also held accountable for many instructional leadership tasks. Principals are responsible for being both the operational leader *and* instructional leader. The job is incredibly different. Education leaders Lee Alvoid and Watt Lesley Black Jr. (2014) state:

> In the public mind, principals were often thought of as mere school-building managers, individuals who were more interested in wielding power and enforcing compliance than in the loftier concerns of teaching and learning.
>
> Today, however, those stale notions could not be further from the truth. The job of a modern-day principal has transformed into something that would be almost unrecognizable to the principals of the 1960s, 1970s, and 1980s. The concept of the principal as a building manager has given way to a model where the principal is an aspirational leader, a team builder, a coach, and an agent of visionary change. (p. 1)

Principals of today were not told they no longer needed to worry about the operations part of the job or that they just need to focus on the instructional aspects. Principals are responsible for the instructional in addition to operational expectations. A principal's job has evolved to carry many more responsibilities and pressures.

In fact, principals today are also required to be *transformational leaders*—in other words, to be principals who can inspire their teachers to go beyond the general expectations of the job to achieve the school's vision and mission. A principal who is a transformational leader empowers and inspires others to be innovative and proactive.

Consider the following aspects of the principal's job that have changed over time and which now pose increased challenges to the work.

> » **Technology:** With the rise of social media, people have access to unreliable information. This means sometimes principals can't get accurate information out in time to counteract gossip, allowing social media rumors to be the dominant narrative. It also means events principals once handled in private are now subject to public

scrutiny—such as a video of students fighting or a recording of a confidential meeting.

» **Accountability:** Principals are responsible for the school's data—such as student achievement, student discipline, teacher retention rates, school climate, and so on—which can easily become public information. These data points reflect the school's leadership (in other words, the school principal). Principals are held accountable for not only school data but also decisions. Whether the decision is to suspend a student or change a bell schedule, the public has the unprecedented ability to hold principals accountable for the outcomes of their decisions.

» **School safety:** School safety conditions have changed drastically since the beginning of the 20th century. There have been almost four hundred school shootings in the United States since the Columbine High School shooting in 1999, which has caused school safety to become school leaders' number one priority (Lynch, 2023). When schools receive threats from students who are planning to harm themselves or others, the principal is immediately responsible for conducting a thorough investigation and handling the results of that investigation. These are threats the principal cannot put off or evaluate later. The community expects the principal to deal with safety threats immediately; everything else on the principal's agenda for that day takes a back seat.

These changing factors place increasing responsibility on principals and make their work ever more challenging. This leaves principals unable to lead their school effectively without support. To successfully meet their responsibilities, principals need the help of teacher leaders. Leadership advisers David Lancefield and Christian Rangen (2021) write, "Successful transformation requires harnessing the leadership team's and organization's collective intelligence, energy, and experience. The degree of change and demands of the effort are too big to leave to an individual."

With the numerous and complex responsibilities for school leaders, it is just not a realistic expectation that one single individual can lead and manage it all (DuFour & Marzano, 2011). With all the added pressures and changes, principals *need* more leaders in the building to help lead this important work for students. According to education researchers Jianping Shen and colleagues (2020), "School improvement is complex work, and principals, alone, are not able to achieve and sustain the expected levels of school improvement."

The Teacher Leadership Exploratory Consortium (n.d.) confirms that teacher leaders can enhance the capacity of principals, noting that collaboration between teacher leaders and school administrators strengthens school leadership:

> Teachers in leadership roles work in collaboration with principals and other school administrators by facilitating improvements in instruction and promoting practices among their peers that can lead to improved student learning outcomes. By doing so, they support school leaders in encouraging innovation and creating cultures of success in school. Teacher leadership can neither be effective nor successful without principal support, but neither can the principal maximize his or her effectiveness without harnessing the talents and expertise of teachers in leadership roles. (p. 11)

Educational consultant Bill Hall's (2022) *Powerful Guiding Coalitions: How to Build and Sustain the Leadership Team in Your PLC at Work* describes the advantages of leading through shared leadership by working in collaboration with other teacher leaders versus a principal who leads alone. Table 1.1 shows a side-by-side comparison of collaborative leadership versus lone leadership.

TABLE 1.1: Collaborative Leadership Versus Lone Leadership

Collaborative Leadership	Leadership by a Lone Leader
Leadership is leveraged. The team shoulders the responsibility so there is less weight for an individual leader to carry.	This leadership takes an enormous amount of energy. One person shoulders all the leadership weight; leadership is not shared or leveraged.
Multiple leaders offer and consider multiple perspectives.	A single perspective limits options and ideas.
Responsibilities can rotate among team members; when one team member is unavailable, another can pitch in or step up.	Leaders are on call 24/7; they have no backups or alternates, and no downtime to recharge, regroup, or re-energize.
Teams can efficiently develop replicable processes and create systems that can last over time; leadership practices are sustainable regardless of who is on the team.	A replicable process to sustain leadership capacity-building may be difficult to create with a lone leader; if the lone leader leaves, there is no one to pick up the torch.
Collaborative leadership builds capacity and re-energizes teams.	Lone leadership can drain energy, does not build capacity, and can deplete the leader's stamina.

Source: Adapted from Hall, 2022.

Benefits of Shared Leadership

When educators think about no longer having one person in charge of leading every-thing, they often refer to the term *shared leadership*—meaning the principal is not the sole leader of the school but shares the leadership role with teacher leaders. Business marketing writer Marisa Sanfilippo (2023) explains it this way: "Shared leadership is more of a collaborative effort. One person is still in charge, but power and influence are shared within the group." The principal shares that power and influence with teacher leaders so everyone is ultimately responsible for leading the school toward student achievement. When school and district leaders initially embrace the PLC work and then abandon it because they don't see results, it's usually due to the lack of shared leadership. In other words, when examining what went wrong in the PLC implementation process, the answer could be a lack of shared leadership. Adjunct professor in educational leadership Terry Wilhelm (2017) writes about this dynamic:

> But there are also great numbers of schools where teachers report, "We tried that at our school, and it didn't work." The missing component? Shared leadership. New initiatives—including PLCs—are mandated constantly from districts, states, and the federal government, but they come and go. Teachers call them pendulum swings. By contrast, shared leadership brings ownership, and ownership brings a lasting commitment to continuous improvement on the part of those who work, day in and day out, teaching the students, in the classrooms of your school.

Shared leadership is critical to PLC work. Without shared leadership, becoming a PLC is nearly impossible. Take a closer look at the advantages of shared leadership in a PLC in the next sections.

Increased Job Satisfaction

Educators know collaboration is the heart and soul of PLCs, so it makes sense that shared leadership is a requirement in a PLC. In a PLC, principals, assistant principals, and teacher leaders work together on the school's leadership team. One of the benefits to shared leadership is empowerment, which leads to job satisfaction (Sanfilippo, 2023). When teacher leaders feel empowered to do the things they know need to happen (and without having to be told what to do), they are more satisfied in their work. Education researchers Victoria Boyd-Dimock and Kathleen M. McGree (n.d.) explain: "Studies have shown that leadership positions can yield significant personal benefits to those involved. Intellectual and professional growth and decreased isolation are personal gains teachers reported in their new leadership roles."

Ownership

As teachers gain the tools they need to lead their colleagues well, they experience a sense of ownership, which can lead to intrinsic motivation. In fact, Sanfilippo (2023) writes about internal motivation as one of the benefits of shared leadership: "When individuals feel they impact the organization and have some power and responsibility, they have a greater desire for success. Goals become more personal to them, and people naturally work harder at anything in which they're personally invested." When teacher leaders experience this investment in their school, they are more likely to become more dedicated to achieving their goals. Think of the impact that could have on student achievement. It's not just the principal who is invested in the goals, but a group of teacher leaders as well: "People care about the success of endeavors they actually lead" (Wilhelm, 2017).

Collective Intelligence

Of course among the biggest advantages to shared leadership is the *collective intelligence*—the knowledge that emerges from a team, which doesn't exist at the individual level—and expertise that a principal receives (Organizational Psychology Degrees, n.d.). The collective team IQ is higher and more developed than any individual person's IQ. Imagine the ideas and solutions collective intelligence generates! Knowledge sharing tends to increase the collaboration in the organization, which results in more innovative and creative ideas. This type of collaboration is more likely to challenge the status quo because multiple leaders work together using their expertise and skill set to support student achievement. Similar to collective intelligence is the multiplier effect.

The Multiplier Effect

Researcher and executive adviser Liz Wiseman (2017) investigated the *concept of multipliers* or when leaders multiply the intelligence around them instead of diminishing peers' intelligence. Wiseman (2017) writes: "Multipliers are genius makers. What we mean by that is that they make everyone around them smarter and more capable. Multipliers invoke each person's unique intelligence and create an atmosphere of genius" (p. 10). The benefits of shared leadership include enabling the principal to be a multiplier. When principals practice shared leadership, they are more likely to exhibit the traits of a multiplier. Successful leaders believe the best in their teammates, recognize each member's genius, and are therefore able to get out of colleagues' way to let them lead.

Proximity to the Work

Because teachers are in the classroom working directly with students daily, they bring a unique and vital perspective to shared leadership the principal cannot access alone. Teacher leaders are closer to the work than the school principal, which means they can see things from a different perspective, and that perspective is important when the principal is trying to implement a PLC:

> Principals who lead PLCs never forget that they cannot do it alone, and so before attempting to persuade an entire faculty to support the PLC process, they identify and recruit highly respected, key staff members to help them champion that process. (DuFour & DuFour, 2012, p. 8)

By being in the classroom, teacher leaders have a unique view that can help principals, who have likely been removed from the classroom for several years.

Leadership Development

By implementing a shared leadership model, school principals have an opportunity to tap into the leadership potential in others they may not have noticed otherwise. By collaborating with teacher leaders and empowering them to lead, principals advertently or inadvertently create future school administrators. This collaboration creates increased opportunities for teacher leaders to consider interest in school administration—something they may not have ever considered if they didn't have a leadership opportunity. Additionally, teacher leaders are not just hired into a school administrator role but trained and developed to organically become school administrators.

Skills Needed for Teacher Leaders

Principals cannot achieve the goals of a PLC without sharing the burden of leadership. In the introduction (see page 1), you learned that a PLC aims to ensure all students learn at high levels. To achieve this ambitious goal, the principal relies on teacher leaders to share the responsibilities of school-improvement initiatives.

Teacher leaders in a PLC influence others on their teams or departments to do the necessary work. Educators and coauthors Kenneth C. Williams and Tom Hierck (2015) write, "Every single person in your organization has the potential to influence others" (p. 18). However, to influence others, teacher leaders must have a specific skill set or competencies. Williams and Hierck (2015) identify six competencies teacher leaders must exhibit to successfully implement a PLC:

1. Challenges the status quo
2. Builds trust through clear communications and expectations
3. Creates a commonly owned plan for success
4. Focuses on team over self
5. Has a high sense of urgency for change and sustainable results
6. Commits to continuous self-improvement (p. 25)

When examining this list, consider the specific leadership skills teacher leaders need to exhibit the six competencies. For example, teacher leaders need courage to challenge the status quo. They need communication skills to build trust. They need self-confidence to commit to continuous self-improvement. All of the competencies are the result of specific leadership skills school leaders must develop in teacher leaders first.

Strengthening a teacher leader's ability to lead is a key component of a successful PLC:

> Leading this work requires a results-driven mindset and deep understanding of how to create necessary cultural shifts. And most importantly, deep implementation of the PLC process happens or *does not* happen, depending on leadership. In fact, we argue that leadership is the number one determining factor in school success. (Spiller & Power, 2022, p. 2)

Former educators Jeanne Spiller and Karen Power (2022), coauthors of *Leading Beyond Intention: Six Areas to Deepen Reflection and Planning in Your PLC at Work*, identify six leadership areas important for PLC leaders to cultivate:

1. Bravely leading from within
2. Leading with coaching
3. Leading through conflict and change
4. Leading change with accountability
5. Going the extra mile (and looking after yourself)
6. Learning always and from everywhere (p. 4)

When examining these leadership areas, you can again see how this list relates to specific leadership skills. For example, to bravely lead from within, leaders must develop courage. To lead through conflict and change, leaders must develop conflict-resolution and change-management skills.

Teacher leaders need a specific set of skills for successful leadership in a PLC (Spiller & Power, 2022; Williams & Hierck, 2015). These two approaches have commonalities and differences. I provide both lists here to demonstrate that a clearly defined list of skills for teacher leaders in a PLC is helpful. Using the ten leadership skills in this book, school leadership teams can build robust professional learning for staff. Teacher leaders don't naturally focus on developing these skills the way principals do. Yet teacher leaders need these skills to influence their colleagues to effectively engage in PLC work. Therefore, it is up to school principals to help teacher leaders develop these skills.

Ten Key Skills of Successful Teacher Leaders

Imagine the ideal teacher leader in your school or district. What are those specific leadership skills you would want to see in all your teacher leaders so they can effectively lead their colleagues? Table 1.2 lists the ten leadership skills of successful teacher leaders.

TABLE 1.2: Ten Key Skills of Successful Teacher Leaders

Internal (Personal) Leadership	External (Team) Leadership
1. Self-confidence	6. Change leadership
2. Courage	7. Innovation
3. Conflict resolution	8. Decision making
4. Lifelong learning	9. Problem solving
5. Emotional intelligence	10. Communication

If school and district leaders help teacher leaders develop these ten leadership skills, they will be well equipped to effectively lead the work of a PLC. Imagine what an asset well-equipped teacher leaders are to a school principal. When shared leadership is successful, it dramatically expands a principal's capacity to advance the work of the PLC.

Summary

When expected to lead PLC work, principals cannot do it in isolation. In fact, working in isolation is the opposite of the PLC premise. When you consider the many responsibilities and pressures that today's principals face, it's clear shared leadership is necessary to the success of a PLC. However, shared leadership begins with accepting the responsibility of developing teacher leaders' leadership skills. Principals cannot expect teacher leaders to lead their colleagues without investing in them first by providing the training they need to strengthen their leadership skills.

REPRODUCIBLE

Reflect on Developing Shared Leadership

Pause to reflect on what you've read in this chapter. Use the following prompts to journal about what you learned and next steps you'll take.

Before reading this chapter, what prior knowledge did you have regarding the relationship between PLCs and shared leadership?

After reading this chapter, what did you learn about shared leadership in a PLC?

What actions will you take to continuously strengthen shared leadership on your campus?

CHAPTER 2

How to Overcome Barriers to Teacher Leadership

In chapter 1, I established *why* shared leadership is so critical for schools, but educators must acknowledge there are some barriers that prevent principals from creating a shared leadership structure and teacher leaders from wanting that shared leadership structure. Districts can mandate that principals develop shared leadership as a best practice, but there are reasons why that might not be as easy as it sounds. Anticipating potential barriers is an important part of implementing any new initiative.

Consider how the common barriers I identify in this chapter relate to your context. Might these barriers shed light on reasons teacher leaders are not really leading in your school? More importantly, focus on the solutions. Might one of these solutions work for your school? Continuous improvement is "baked into" the culture of a PLC. In other words, an inherent part of your work in a PLC is identifying those barriers that hinder your ability to make things better, and creating viable solutions to overcome them.

I begin this chapter by naming four common barriers to shared leadership. These include (1) leadership style, (2) role confusion, (3) peer attitudes, and (4) time. I spend the rest of the chapter examining how you can overcome these barriers.

Common Barriers to Shared Leadership

What are some common barriers principals face when establishing a culture of shared leadership? In the following sections I examine how leadership style, role confusion, peer attitudes, and time pose particular challenges.

Leadership Style

Sometimes principals' default approach to leadership poses a barrier to creating a shared leadership culture at their school. This can manifest in micromanaging and other ineffective leadership approaches. This leadership style is the opposite of Wiseman's (2017) multipliers, or what she calls "diminishers" (p. xvii). Principals who are *diminishers* feel the need to do everything themselves because they believe others are just not "smart enough" to do it. These leaders micromanage because they lack confidence in their staff's capabilities and intelligence. They not only feel the need to do everything themselves but also control everything others do. Forbes Coaches Council (2020) states that leaders who are micromanagers typically lack trust in their staff, must have the last word, always check on work progress, redo the teams' work, and spend more time on how others complete the work than on the outcome. Unfortunately, this behavior is unsustainable, undermines PLC culture, and fails to accomplish the goal of shared leadership.

Micromanaging isn't the only quality that sidelines principals. Researchers Maria Brown and David Ringwood (2021) identify five blocks to shared leadership in their study.

1. High emphasis on making decisions independently and working autonomously

2. High emphasis on being competitive, authoritative, and forceful

3. Low emphasis on delegating and then giving others freedom to learn without interference

4. Low emphasis on helping others and putting the team's interests first

5. Low emphasis on seeking opinions from others and adopting their ideas, encouraging democracy

Brown and Ringwood (2021) find when leaders have three or more of these blockers, they impact the leaders' ability to lead effectively because they are less collaborative. For example, these types of leaders are less likely to request and accept input from others, less likely to delegate, and more likely to make decisions independently.

Insecurities can also play a role with all leaders and their leadership style. Insecure school principals may fear their teacher leaders will outperform or outshine them. Insecure principals manage people through intimidation, have a closed "Do what I say" attitude, may not like feedback, focus only on their own successes, and play favorites to those who will "kiss up to the principal" (Reid, 2022).

When teacher leaders are insecure, they may shy away from taking necessary action or advocating for change for fear of inciting conflict or dislike from others. They prefer to keep the status quo and are more concerned about what their colleagues think than what is best for the school or students. Whether the principal or the teacher leader is battling insecurity, the outcome is the same: insecurities can prevent school leaders from developing a shared leadership culture.

Principals will inevitably have different leadership styles, but a principal committed to establishing shared leadership must embrace skills that foster that initiative. If those skills are missing, principals must first focus on cultivating their own shared leadership model with the help of a coach or mentor. Otherwise, the principals' leadership style could be the biggest barrier to implementing shared leadership.

Role Confusion

Confusion about the teacher leader's role poses a barrier to successful shared leadership. Typically, teacher leaders look to former teacher leaders to see what they did and then do the same. This often means they function as an intermediary, sharing information with teachers from meetings with the principal and vice versa. Basically, they are the "in-between" person who relays communication between teachers in the department or team and school administrators. So instead of being teacher leaders, they are more *teacher representatives* or *teacher advocates*.

This means that traditionally, teacher leaders weren't *leading*. They may have the title *leader*, but they don't stand alongside the principal to bear the burden of responsibility that a shared leadership model demands. When teacher leaders are confused as to their role, or if principals are even confused as to what the teacher leaders' role is, it makes it difficult to do the job effectively.

In a PLC, clarity is paramount, including clarity with roles. If professionals working in a PLC don't have clarity about their role, they lack focus, and will likely struggle to work at peak capacity and relate successfully to their teammates. Imagine team members who aren't sure who is responsible for facilitating meetings, recording minutes, and so on. The team would waste much time outlining those tasks before the meeting could begin. Teacher leaders need to know what their role entails, and how school leaders expect them to complete their assigned duties. Without that clarity, principals and teacher leaders will be confused, unsure what to do, and insecure in relating to one another in a culture of shared leadership.

In their article about teacher leadership, Boyd-Dimock and McGree (n.d.) write, "When responsibilities involved with leadership are not well delineated confusion results and tensions mount, not only for lead teachers but also for those who work with them (i.e., administrators, classroom teachers)."

Peer Attitudes

Teacher leaders frequently struggle to meet the demands of school leaders because of peers' negative attitudes. Educational leader Meena Wilson (1993) notes, "The very capabilities that distinguish teacher leaders from others . . .—risk-taking, collaboration, and role modeling—produce tensions between them and colleagues" (p. 26). Regardless of whether this attitude is real or perceived, it poses a barrier for teacher leaders to truly lead in the shared leadership model. Some teacher leaders may believe their peers do not like them in the leadership role and, as a result, try to minimize their own role.

This dynamic is apparent in educational research. After interviewing teacher leaders, educational consultant Lynn F. Zinn (1997) finds that the participants in her study:

> Feel a number of teachers resent them, their success, and their visibility. Lea's close working relationship with her former and current principals is resented by some of her colleagues. . . . Maya describes resentment of colleagues, as a result of her close working relationship with her princi-pal. She states, "Sometimes, you're seen as a person who has the ear of the principal . . . a teacher's pet kind of thing. And I think that plays a role in the perceptions of colleagues in the building." (p. 12)

This perception of favoritism can really impact how colleagues view teacher leaders. Relationships with colleagues are important to teacher leaders; if they feel their role as a leader creates tensions among colleagues, teacher leaders may step down from the role.

The attitudes of fellow teachers can easily become a barrier to successfully creating a shared leadership culture.

Time

Most teacher leaders still teach and may even have a full load of classes. Being a teacher leader requires a lot of time outside the classroom. This impacts their ability to not only lead but also teach effectively: "With additional responsibilities and little extra time, teachers are often forced to make sacrifices that compromise their ability to be effective in both roles" (Boyd-Dimock & McGree, n.d.). Zinn (1997) reports the following barriers in relationship to time for teacher leaders:

- Too much to do in the available time.
- Lack of time to work collegially.
- Classroom responsibilities limit available time. (p. 38)

Because teacher leaders are still responsible for teaching, it is difficult for them to ignore that responsibility to take on leading their colleagues' responsibilities, or do both jobs well. Principals who anticipate time as a barrier may have low expectations of teacher leaders to begin with because they're trying to be aware of teacher leaders' capacity.

Now that you know some of the barriers principals and teacher leaders face in embracing a shared leadership model, I'll examine some possible solutions.

Address Leadership Style

How can principals overcome the barriers of unsupportive leadership skills like micromanaging, insecurity, and diminishing? *Diminishers* drain intelligence from the people around them, while *multipliers* magnify the intelligence and capabilities of the people around them (Wiseman, 2017).

A great first step is to determine your readiness (as the principal) to adopt a shared leadership culture. If you find yourself in this position, determining your readiness will help you identify what specific areas of building shared leadership pose a challenge for you. Engaging in self-reflection will support you to identify and address ways in which your leadership style might pose a barrier to successful shared leadership. Figure 2.1 (page 26) offers a self-evaluation tool principals can use to determine their readiness to build teacher leaders.

Directions: Read each statement; then check *yes* or *no* to indicate whether you currently exhibit the leadership behavior. In the far-right column, write reflections about your strengths and opportunities for growth related to each behavior. Remember, this is a reflective tool. It will be most beneficial if you base your reflection on your reality rather than your (or other people's) ideal.

Leading Change

	Yes	No	Reflections
I understand the importance of collaborating with key stakeholders to shape a vision of academic success for my school.	☐	☐	
I know how to engage others in school-improvement efforts.	☐	☐	
I know what leadership gaps to fill to achieve school-improvement goals.	☐	☐	
I have the ability to assess the strengths and weaknesses of staff.	☐	☐	
I can identify individuals who possess the right combination of skill and will to fill leadership gaps.	☐	☐	
I am equipped to overcome challenges related to creating new leadership roles in my school.	☐	☐	

Communicating Effectively

	Yes	No	Reflections
I understand the importance of two-way communication.	☐	☐	
I build communication processes that make it safe for people to say what is on their minds.	☐	☐	
I listen to others actively, checking to ensure my understanding.	☐	☐	
I am willing to change my viewpoint based on the valid opinions of others.	☐	☐	
I work to understand others' perspectives.	☐	☐	

Developing People			
	Yes	No	Reflections
I have built the climate for teachers to play a role in making key decisions.	☐	☐	
I feel confident enough to let others assume leadership roles.	☐	☐	
I help people take advantage of opportunities to learn new skills.	☐	☐	
I know how to scaffold leadership opportunities for teachers.	☐	☐	
I know how to manage teacher leader workload to avoid burnout.	☐	☐	
I know how to provide effective performance feedback.	☐	☐	
I celebrate progress related to the school vision.	☐	☐	

Source: Adapted from Georgia Leadership Institute for School Improvement (GLISI), 2015.

FIGURE 2.1: Readiness to build teacher leaders self-assessment.

*Visit **go.SolutionTree.com/PLCbooks** for a free reproducible of this figure.*

If you find several areas you need to work on, focus on those areas. Did you identify leading change, communicating effectively, developing people, or another area of growth? In the Reflections column, you should reflect on not only the *why* but also your next steps. Create actionable next steps to ensure you will get stronger in that particular area. You can use the guidance in part 2 (page 47) to help you, as it's worthwhile for principals in addition to teacher leaders.

Address Role Confusion

For principals to develop shared leadership on their campus, a key first step is defining their role within a culture of shared leadership. Sometimes principals are willing to embrace shared leadership in their school but make missteps along the way because they don't understand what *shared leadership* means or looks like. They may wonder, "What am I responsible for leading if I'm empowering teacher leaders to lead?"

Shared leadership doesn't necessarily mean giving up all your power and control and letting teacher leaders do everything. It's about finding the right balance within the dynamic of shared responsibility: "As the term *shared* implies, shared leadership does involve sharing some decision making and other responsibilities, but it is not abdication, and it is quite different from simple delegation" (Wilhelm, 2013).

In an article for *Harvard Business Review*, executive leadership coach and author Marshall Goldsmith (2010) argues that global expansion calls for organizations to become more flexible, disperse power, and share leadership with team members based on their areas of expertise. Goldsmith (2010) offers the following suggestions for sharing leadership and maximizing talent (see figure 2.2). Review these suggestions and indicate in the right column how each relates to your experience of defining the role of the principal in developing teacher leaders.

Instructions: Review Goldsmith's (2010) suggestions and take notes about what each might look like in your context.	
Suggestions for sharing leadership and maximizing talent (Goldsmith, 2010)	**My role in creating a culture of shared leadership**
"Give power away to the most qualified individuals to strengthen their capabilities."	
"Define the limits of decision-making power."	
"Cultivate a climate in which people feel free to take initiative on assignments."	
"Give qualified people discretion and autonomy over their tasks and resources and encourage them to use these tools."	
"Don't second guess the decisions of those you empowered to do so."	
"Consider yourself a resource rather than the manager."	
"Set appropriate follow-up meetings to review progress and take corrective action if necessary."	

Source: Adapted from Goldsmith, 2020.

FIGURE 2.2: Defining the principal's role.

Visit go.SolutionTree.com/PLCbooks for a free reproducible of this figure.

Just like the principal has a significant role to play in building a culture of shared leadership, so do teacher leaders.

In their executive summary, leadership training organization New Leaders (2015b) notes the four high-impact leadership domains their Emerging Leaders Program (ELP;

a job-embedded leadership development program for teachers) targets. These are essentially the roles school leaders expect teacher leaders to perform:

1. **Instructional Leadership:** Setting high expectations for all students, applying content expertise, leading data-driven instruction and coaching teachers.
2. **Personal Leadership:** Receiving feedback and self-reflecting to continuously improve performance and instruction.
3. **Culture Leadership:** Building expectations, systems and incentives to promote urgency and efficacy among adults to improve student achievement.
4. **Adult Leadership:** Communicating skillfully, motivating a team, giving constructive feedback and facilitating effective meetings. (New Leaders, 2015b, p. 2)

Notice how these four domains in the ELP program clarify the role of teacher leaders; the role is no longer abstract or ambiguous. Bringing clarity to teacher leaders' roles could involve working with teacher leaders to brainstorm what specific tasks they will take on and behaviors they will exhibit within each domain. Use figure 2.3 to take notes as needed.

Instructions: Review New Leaders' (2015b) high-impact leadership domains and take notes about what your role and responsibilities might look like in your context.	
New Leaders' (2015b) high-impact leadership domains	**My role and responsibilities in creating a culture of shared leadership**
"**Instructional Leadership:** Setting high expectations for all students, applying content expertise, leading data-driven instruction, and coaching teachers."	
"**Personal Leadership:** Receiving feedback and self-reflecting to continuously improve performance and instruction."	
"**Culture Leadership:** Building expectations, systems and incentives to promote urgency and efficacy among adults to improve student achievement."	
"**Adult Leadership:** Communicating skillfully, motivating a team, giving constructive feedback, and facilitating effective meetings."	

Source: Adapted from New Leaders, 2015b.

FIGURE 2.3: Defining the teacher leader's role.

*Visit **go.SolutionTree.com/PLCbooks** for a free reproducible of this figure.*

Another way to bring clarity to the teacher leaders' job is by discussing table 2.1 with leaders on your campus. This chart outlines the differences between the roles of teacher leaders in a traditional school leadership team and in a PLC school leadership team.

TABLE 2.1: Role of Teacher Leaders in a Traditional Versus PLC School Leadership Team

Traditional School Leadership Team	PLC School Leadership Team
Communicates information from the principal back to their teachers	Leads their teachers
Takes issues and concerns from the teachers to their principal	Problem solves with the teachers and takes the solutions to their principal
Advocates for the teachers	Advocates for the students the department or team serves
Waits for direction from the principal before acting	Takes initiative and takes action as needed
Focuses on being the best classroom teachers to continue being on the leadership team	Focuses on growing the teachers to have the best department or team
Does not believe it's their job to have tough conversations with their teachers	Believes in having tough conversations with their teachers when needed
Believes having the *principal* title would help them lead their teachers	Believes they can lead with or without a title
Focuses on teachers liking them	Focuses on advancing the school's mission statement
Contributes to morale issues by staying quiet (or agreeing) when complaints and negativity come up	Sets a positive tone in their team and department by addressing the complaints and negativity as they come up
Loyalty is to their teachers	Loyalty is to their school

These are just two among many possible ways of clarifying the role of teacher leaders. There's no right or sanctioned way to do this; the point is, it's an essential step. Without that clarification, teachers will continue to operate in their traditional role:

> We [teachers] can't see that a lack of clarity is the root cause behind everything from poor productivity to personal conflict. We don't realize that we can't *cruise with confidence* if we don't know *exactly* what we are trying to accomplish, how, and with whom. We don't recognize that a lack of specificity, focus, and clearly-defined process is eroding progress every step of the way. (Latham, 2021a)

If you're not sure how to begin this step on your campus, use table 2.1 to start the conversation with your teacher leaders. Work together to construct a job description or a teacher leader roles and responsibilities chart tailored to your campus.

By involving teacher leaders in this process, you have an opportunity to talk through, unpack, and understand what the teacher leaders' role is in a shared leadership model. For example, educational leaders Cindy Harrison and Joellen Killion (2007) share the following roles for teacher leaders.

» Resource provider

» Instructional specialist

» Curriculum specialist

» Classroom supporter

» Learning facilitator

» Mentor

» School leader

» Data coach

» Catalyst for change

» Learner

As a team, you can add to this list and then define what each responsibility looks like for teacher leaders. After completing your teacher leader job description, share that final product with the entire staff. The entire staff also needs clarity and a good understanding of what teacher leaders do at their school, including the teacher leaders' responsibilities.

Figure 2.4 (page 32) shows a sample teacher leaders' roles and responsibilities chart.

Instructional Teacher Leaders	Operational Teacher Leaders
• Provide professional development to teachers.	• Plan morale boosters (birthdays, celebrations, and so on).
• Review collaborative team minutes and products.	• Schedule student recognitions.
• Mentor new teachers.	• Approve discipline referrals before they go to an administrator.
• Monitor teacher blogs and websites.	• Organize field trips.
• Lead the PLC work.	• Coordinate substitute teachers.
• Model professional behavior.	• Model professional behavior.
• Respect and love our school.	• Respect and love our school.
• Support administrators.	• Support administrators.

FIGURE 2.4: Sample teacher leaders' roles and responsibilities chart.

*Visit **go.SolutionTree.com/PLCbooks** for a free reproducible of this figure.*

During their conversations, this team recognizes there are operational responsibilities as well as instructional responsibilities to clarify. More importantly, they recognize that teacher leaders each have different desires and skill sets that complement one another. This is the genius of a shared leadership culture—maximizing talent and increasing capacity.

Address Peer Attitudes

Once teacher leaders embrace their role of truly leading, their colleagues sometimes resist the change. Teacher leaders need support in handling their peers during this transition.

One way to address this challenge is to spread leadership opportunities to multiple teachers to avoid favoritism. Establish a rule that teacher leaders on the school's leadership team are not allowed to volunteer for any other leadership opportunities. For example, if the principal has a school climate committee, it would consist of different teacher leaders than the safety committee. Providing diverse opportunities to lead different initiatives helps spread the leadership rather than the traditional practice of a select group of teacher leaders in the school taking on all leadership tasks.

Transparency is another way of avoiding negative peer attitudes. Once you have clarified teacher leaders' roles, communicate that information to the entire staff. Everyone in the school should know exactly what teacher leaders are responsible for doing; their job description should not be a secret. Transparency on the role of teacher leaders can help other teachers understand the role better.

Finally, it might help just having conversations with prospective and new teacher leaders about how their new leadership role could impact their relationships with their colleagues. Offering new teacher leaders suggestions for working through the transition helps support them. Following are some suggestions for your teacher leaders.

» Schedule one-to-one meetings with each teacher on your team to acknowledge your role as the teacher leader and ask what you can do to support each teacher with this transition.

» Provide opportunities for shared leadership within your department and team, considering how you can grow more teacher leaders. Invest in your teachers the way your principal is investing in you.

» Discuss boundaries. Consider what steps you will take to establish boundaries with the teachers in your department or team.

Address Time

How can principals maximize teacher leaders' time? Knowing teacher leaders have more on their plate, think about things you can do to support teacher leaders to make the most of their time.

If providing supplemental pay is not an option in your district, consider offering an additional planning period. If extra planning time isn't available, consider providing collaboration opportunities so teacher leaders can have *thought partners* to think through things with and share the load. Ideally, this happens during teacher leadership meetings. How can principals plan their teacher leadership meetings to provide time for teacher leaders to collaborate with one another about leadership?

As time-consuming as it is to fulfill all the roles of a teacher leader, the most important uses of time are teacher leadership meetings. Those meetings should be incredibly valuable in helping support teacher leaders. Start teacher leadership meetings with professional development activities that support development of the ten key leadership skills (see page 19), such as the activities in part 2 (page 47). When you leave professional development to the end of the meeting, there is a high probability you won't get to it. Figure 2.5 (page 34) shows a sample school leadership meeting agenda. Notice that professional development is first on the agenda, leaving the operational or managerial items to the end of the meeting.

Professional Development	
How do you strengthen your meeting facilitation skills?	
What best practices should happen at the beginning of every meeting?	
What best practices should happen during every meeting?	
What best practices should happen at the end of every meeting?	
Instructional Agenda	
What do we want teachers to learn?	*Instructional strategies: develop professional learning plan for teachers*
How do we know if teachers have learned it?	*Not applicable*
What do we do as a school when teachers don't learn it?	*Not applicable*
What do we do as a school when teachers do learn it?	*Not applicable*
Managerial Agenda	
Teacher attendance	
Chain of command with front office	
School-improvement team focus	

FIGURE 2.5: Sample school leadership meeting agenda.

Leadership meetings should make developing key leadership skills a top priority. Professional development should always be first on the agenda because that is the most important thing a principal can do—develop their teacher leaders to lead effectively. Operational and managerial concerns should be at the end.

Summary

It is easy to jump right into a shared leadership initiative, but taking stock of obstacles and designing solutions is essential to successful implementation. Examining their leadership styles and strengthening weak areas empowers principals to create a shared leadership structure that micromanaging or insecurities won't sabotage. Clarifying the roles and responsibilities of the principal and teacher leaders will head off confusion about team dynamics and task allocation. Additionally, supporting teacher leaders to manage negative peer attitudes and bids for their time contributes to the success of shared leadership structures. While these barriers are common on many campuses, each school will face its own unique challenges. Ultimately, principals and teacher leaders must rely on the second big idea of a PLC—collaborative culture and collective responsibility—to guide them through the process. Work together to identify and overcome barriers your team faces to successfully implement a shared leadership structure.

Reflect on Addressing Barriers to Shared Leadership

Pause to reflect on what you've read in this chapter. Use the following prompts to journal about what you learned and next steps you'll take.

What prior knowledge did you have regarding the barriers that prevent you from having a true shared leadership model?

After reading this chapter, what did you learn about barriers to implementing shared leadership and probable solutions?

To strengthen shared leadership on your campus, what are your barriers and how will you resolve them?

CHAPTER 3

How to Select Teacher Leaders

After clarifying the role of teacher leader, now it's time to consider the process for selecting teacher leaders.

Typically, there are four strategies administrators use to select teacher leaders: (1) put out a call to the entire staff asking for volunteers, (2) ask specific teachers to serve, (3) ask retiring teacher leaders to find their successor, and (4) employ a formal application and interview process.

Response to intervention (RTI) experts Austin Buffum, Mike Mattos, and Janet Malone (2018), coauthors of *Taking Action: A Handbook for RTI at Work*, note the importance of careful consideration when choosing teacher leaders:

> We find it both fascinating and tragic that many schools give more careful consideration to forming their varsity football coaching staff or school social committee than to forming the best possible school guiding coalition. Random practices, such as the following, often determine positions on the school leadership team.
> - **Seniority:** "I should be department chair because I have been here the longest."
> - **Novice:** "Make the rookie do it. Pay your dues, kid!"
> - **Rotation:** "It's Sally's turn to be grade-level leader."
> - **Default:** "Bill is the only person who applied." (pp. 36–37)

When Williams and Hierck (2015) asked school leaders how they select teacher leaders for their leadership teams, they discovered it comes down to "leadership by default" (p. 19). Consider the following scenarios they include in *Starting a Movement: Building Culture From the Inside Out in Professional Learning Communities*:

- "We have a grade-level team of three teachers, Jerry, Linda, and Joan. Joan is the representative from our team on the leadership team this year; Jerry fulfilled that role last year, so it is Linda's turn next."
- "Our leadership team representative receives a stipend to serve on the team. Therefore, we rotate the responsibility from year to year so everyone gets a chance to earn the extra money."
- "We let the principal decide who is on the team and then those people stay on the team until they decide they no longer want the position." (Williams & Hierck, 2015, p. 19)

In this chapter, I review a variety of ways to select teacher leaders to strengthen your school's leadership team for leading the PLC work to ultimately impact student achievement. These methods include selection by interviews, peer identification, four powers, evaluation of leadership skills, and self-evaluations. Next, I examine obstacles principals sometimes face to selecting teacher leaders.

Selection Methods

So, why the ambiguity about how to select teacher leaders? Teacher-Led Professional Learning (n.d.) reports a gap in the research when it comes to providing school administrators with practical guidelines and suggestions on how to select teacher leaders. It is critical that school leaders not only have a clearly defined process for selecting teacher leaders but also a robust one. School leaders need a process that can identify the right teacher leaders to lead the work in collaboration with the school administrators. The following sections present several methods for selecting teacher leaders.

Interviews

One way to identify teacher leaders is through formal interviews in which you assess applicants on their experience and strengths in various areas. Teacher-Led Professional Learning (n.d.) suggests conducting behavioral interviews to select teacher leaders:

> Research suggests that if developed and implemented correctly, behavioral interviews that ask candidates to tell about past events in detail have a high potential to determine if a candidate has the

competencies that are predictive of superior performance in a particular job. The past-event interviewing technique asks candidates to offer examples of how they thought, felt, and acted in the context of a specific, real-life, past situation, rather than asking for their opinions or philosophies about work success.

Think critically about the interview questions you'll ask. Make sure to include the experience-based questions you would expect during a job interview. In addition to asking candidates each what their strengths are, ask questions that allow candidates to share a past experience that demonstrates the particular skills you're looking for in teacher leaders on your team. Consider the following examples of interview questions.

» Describe a time when you had a conflict with a colleague. What was the conflict and how did you resolve it? How would you resolve it as a teacher leader?

» As a member of our school leadership team, you are an extension of the school administration. How will you show your support of the administration and our school this year?

» What are some of your qualities that make you the best choice for this leadership position?

» What are the top two things you would like to change to increase the effectiveness of your department?

» What are some examples of reflective practices you engage in as a teacher? How will those change if you take on the role of teacher leader?

» What specific leadership strength will you bring to the teacher leader role? How do you know it's a strength of yours?

» A teacher leader's job is to advocate for students. How will you support your teachers to ensure students are learning at high levels?

» How will you influence the teachers in your team, department, or grade level?

» What was your last professional learning experience? What changes did you make as a result that have prepared you to be a teacher leader?

» How will you handle challenging group dynamics?

» What steps will you take to design meaningful and effective professional learning opportunities for your teachers?

In addition, consider who you want to include on the interview panel. Would a district leader or current (or past) teacher leader help you identify the best candidate for the position?

Teacher-Led Professional Learning (n.d.) also offers the following guidelines based on cross-sector evidence for selecting teacher leaders:

1. **Demonstrated Job Skills**. Has the individual demonstrated the skills needed to fulfill their job responsibilities?
2. **Observable Behavioral Competencies**. Has the individual demonstrated that (s)he typically uses behavioral competencies— the habits of behavior that help predict how an individual will perform in a job—at the level needed to be effective in this position?
3. **Prior Evidence of Success**. Has the individual proved that (s)he can achieve outcome goals correlated with success in the new role?

These guidelines are useful for those unsure how to begin the selection process. However, school and district leaders must take some preliminary steps first, such as writing the job description for teacher leaders, identifying behavioral competencies you expect of teacher leaders, and naming the evidence of success you'll look for in candidates. This will help you find the right candidates and help clarify the teacher leader role, as I discuss in chapter 2 (page 21).

Peer Identification

Principal Rachel Jones (2015) uses another method to identify teacher leaders in her school: staff surveys, which help her gain insight about educators' leadership potential. This method proved a good fit for Jones (2015) after serving as her school's principal for thirteen years and establishing trust and strong relationships with her teachers.

Using an anonymous survey, Jones (2015) asked her teachers:

- Who, of their colleagues, would be a trusted, critical observer of instruction;
- Who is considered very knowledgeable/successful in math instruction and language arts instruction;
- Who has strong classroom management skills;
- Who has strong technology integration skills; and
- Who teachers would choose to work with in a collaborative team.

Prior to giving this survey, Jones (2015) assured her staff (1) the results were completely anonymous, (2) she would be the only staff member to see these results, and (3) she would not use the surveys for their evaluations. After receiving the survey results, Jones (2015) knew which teachers in leadership positions their peers would receive well.

In addition to identifying potential teacher leaders, this approach offers other benefits. Jones (2015) could identify teachers their peers did *not* select; she used the opportunity to provide those teachers with support and help them set goals for professional growth. In addition, when teachers approached her with an interest in pursuing leadership opportunities, she shared the characteristics their peers looked for in teacher leaders. Finally, filling leadership roles with these peer-identified teachers ensures the school's teacher leaders are capable and effective, and would remain in their positions for a few years (Jones, 2015).

When considering this option for your context, think through the logistics. For example: Will you make the survey anonymous? Is a survey the best choice, or would a voting process work best on your campus? Ask yourself how to adjust the process to best support you in selecting the best teacher leader candidate.

Four Powers

Schools can also select teacher leaders based on four essential types of power (Buffum et al., 2018; Mattos, Buffum, Malone, Cruz, Dimich, & Schuhl, in press). Professor of leadership emeritus John P. Kotter (2012) identifies the following specific powers in his book *Leading Change*.

» **Power of position:** Some teachers on campus already hold leadership positions, such as school climate committee chair, department leader, team facilitator, and so on. Include the teachers already leading a project, initiative, or task on the school's leadership team.

» **Power of expertise:** Staff may know some teachers in your building for having a specific area of expertise, such as literacy or technology. Look for people on staff who have an area of expertise; they are strong candidates for leadership opportunities.

» **Power of credibility:** Some teachers stand out as having credibility. *Merriam-Webster* defines *credibility* (n.d.) as "the quality or power of inspiring belief." Think about the teachers in your school or district who have the ability to inspire belief in others. These are the teachers others trust. These are the natural teacher leaders who other teachers look up to.

» **Power of leadership ability:** Some teachers are natural-born leaders, those who intuitively influence others. You're looking for those teachers who can influence others to believe and take action.

Which of these powers do the teachers on your campus represent? Ideally, you want your leadership team to embody each of these powers to achieve balance and amplify the team's impact. You can use either the interview or peer-identification process to ask candidates questions related to these four powers. Alternatively, as a school or district, conduct an assessment of what leadership powers are missing at your school and only focus on asking questions related to those powers. This will help you find the teacher leaders who have the power your leadership team needs to achieve balance.

Evaluation of Leadership Skills

Another way to select teacher leaders is by evaluating which leadership skills your school needs to move forward. Begin with the list of the ten key leadership skills (see figure 3.1). Just like the powers in the previous section, this method gives you an opportunity to select teacher leaders with a variety of leadership skills, which makes for a robust team. For instance, if your current teacher leaders exhibit strong collaborative skills but are not strong in being courageous, then the next teacher leader you bring to the team may need to have that specific leadership skill as a strength.

Instructions: Consider the following list of leadership skills. Check the box for each skill that currently exists on your team, and take notes to indicate who embodies these skills. What leadership skills are missing on your current school leadership team?	
Leadership Skill	**Notes**
☐ Self-confidence	
☐ Courage	
☐ Conflict resolution	
☐ Lifelong learning	
☐ Emotional intelligence	
☐ Change leadership	
☐ Innovation	
☐ Decision making	
☐ Problem solving	
☐ Communication	

FIGURE 3.1: The ten key leadership skills for PLC leadership teams.

Visit go.SolutionTree.com/PLCbooks for a free reproducible of this figure.

Figure 3.1 is a worksheet you can use to identify the leadership skills currently represented (and those missing) on your school's leadership team. To complete the worksheet, ask current teacher leaders to identify their strengths and areas for growth, and then examine their collective responses to identify which leadership skills you need to represent on your leadership team.

Self-Evaluation

Another technique for selecting teacher leaders is to involve prospective teacher leaders in a self-evaluation process. Use this self-evaluation of leadership skills with prospective teacher leaders so you can see how they view themselves. Figure 3.2 is an example based on the ten leadership skills.

Directions: On a scale of 1–4, rate yourself on each of the following leadership skills. After you complete the rating part of this self-evaluation, use the questions at the end to reflect on the process.				
	1 = Novice	**2 = Developing**	**3 = Proficient**	**4 = Expert**
Self-confidence				
Courage				
Conflict resolution				
Lifelong learning				
Emotional intelligence				
Change leadership				
Innovation				
Decision making				
Problem solving				
Communication				
Reflection • Which leadership skill is a clear strength and why? • Which leadership skill are you developing? How are you developing that skill?				

FIGURE 3.2: Sample self-evaluation for prospective teacher leaders.

Visit **go.SolutionTree.com/PLCbooks** *for a free reproducible of this figure.*

Regardless of what selection criteria or combination of selection criteria you use, the key takeaway is to have a plan for how you will select teacher leaders. Establishing this process will ensure your school selects top talent to play this critical role on the school's leadership team.

Obstacles to Selecting Teacher Leaders

While some principals face the challenge of selecting teacher leaders, others don't have the opportunity to undertake the selection process at all. Many times, school leaders have already identified teacher leaders; in that case, a principal new to the school may not be able to select teacher leaders. In other cases, a veteran principal may find it awkward to suddenly bring on new members to established school leadership teams. However, whether you are a new or veteran principal, you must fill vacant teacher leader positions on your team or you must start from scratch with your school leadership team.

If it is the latter, you will need to weigh the pros and cons of asking teacher leaders to step down from their leadership role. Former teacher, principal, and assistant principal Bill Hall (2022) shares that it is easier to move people out of business roles than school roles. Once you ask teacher leaders to step down from their leadership role, they are still teachers in your school. What would that look like? Hall (2022) suggests principals consider the following questions before making changes to their leadership team:

- Is it worth it to remove these people?
- How might they react?
- Could they possibly cause harm to your collaborative efforts?
- Can you provide unproductive or ill-suited [school leadership] team members with other leadership opportunities? (p. 18)

Finally, if after careful consideration, you decide you cannot remove teacher leaders from their leadership roles, then you have the responsibility for holding them accountable to be the teacher leaders you need them to be. Be sure to first establish clear expectations for the teacher leadership role and then help identify what specific areas members need to develop.

Removing teacher leaders is not the only option. In fact, the best option is to identify the reasons why you would want to remove them and then work on a plan to help them improve those areas. Best-case scenario is you keep all the teachers on your leadership team, but identify what areas each member needs to work on for growth. Then use the guidance and activities in part 2 (page 47) to tailor teacher leaders' training to their specific needs.

Summary

Take the time to prepare your teacher leadership–selection process to ensure you get the best candidates possible to help lead your school. What method is the best fit for your context? I provide several selection methods, so think about selecting one or a combination of a few to establish a process for selecting teacher leaders. Then, consider whether you want district or school leaders to join you on this collaborative effort. Finally, evaluate your current teacher leaders and consider whether you will initiate a professional development plan with them or remove them from the team. A successful shared leadership culture hinges on this kind of intentional approach for selecting teacher leaders.

Reflect on Selecting Teacher Leaders

Pause to reflect on what you've read in this chapter. Use the following prompts to journal about what you learned and next steps you'll take.

What prior knowledge did you have regarding the selection process for teacher leaders?

After reading this chapter, what did you learn about the process of selecting teacher leaders?

What steps will you take to develop a comprehensive teacher leader–selection process?

PART 2

In part 1, you learned *why* shared leadership is necessary in PLCs and how principals can create a culture of shared leadership on their campus. In part 2, you'll learn how to help teacher leaders develop the ten key leadership skills they need to thrive. The most important thing schools can do is to have effective school leadership teams. Work to develop teacher leaders' leadership skills. Too often, principals place teachers in leadership roles without teaching them *how* to lead other teachers. It's tempting to assume they will figure it out. Leading adults is quite different from leading students, so principals have a responsibility to develop and cultivate leadership skills in every teacher leader on their leadership team.

Each chapter in part 2 begins with an overview of the skill and then provides professional learning activities principals can offer teacher leaders striving to grow that skill.

FIGURE P2.1: Profile of a teacher leader in a PLC.

CHAPTER 4

Developing Self-Confidence Skills

There is no question, *self-confidence* is a skill teacher leaders must continuously foster. School and district leaders expect teacher leaders in a PLC to make decisions, take initiative, and influence their colleagues to ensure all students achieve at high levels. All those behaviors require teacher leaders to have self-confidence. Think about it: How will an anxious or indecisive leader inspire teachers to make changes? As a principal, it is your obligation to help teacher leaders develop the self-confidence skills they need to lead their colleagues.

Developing self-confidence is not a destination, but rather an ongoing process. There is never a time when a person feels fully confident and will have that skill for life. Self-confidence is one of those skills that goes up and down throughout a school year. A leader might be feeling confident . . . until receiving an email from an angry parent who questions a decision or a colleague who offers constructive feedback. The key to growing self-confidence is understanding it is an ongoing commitment. Even the most confident people have experiences that make them doubt themselves.

In this chapter, I explore practices to help teacher leaders grow self-confidence over time. Next, I discuss the PLC connection—specifically to big idea number two (collaborative culture and collective responsibility). The chapter ends with a series of professional development activities to support teacher leaders to develop self-confidence.

Practices for Developing Self-Confidence

Self-confidence is a critical skill for any leader to possess. But what is *confidence*? Confidence has nothing to do with whether you actually *have* the capabilities or whether you *think* you do. *Confidence* means as a leader, you *believe* you are capable. Researcher and consultant Ruth H. Axelrod (2017) writes:

> It [self-confidence] is defined as *an individual's level of certainty about his or her ability to handle things.* Self-confidence is formed through complex internal processes of judgement and self-persuasion whereby we attach meaning to our personal experiences—particularly our successes and failures in past performances—and comprehend others' reactions to us. (p. 298)

If teacher leaders are to truly lead their colleagues, they cannot do that without self-confidence (or without the belief that they can lead their colleagues). Confidence empowers teacher leaders to do the following.

- » Communicate effectively with their colleagues.
- » Eradicate self-doubt and take risks.
- » Accept feedback to facilitate growth.
- » Bring a sense of calm to the team.
- » Implement changes with much more success.

Ultimately, confident teacher leaders help school administrators achieve the mission and vision of the school. They are the champions of the work and influence their colleagues *if* they have the self-confidence. Consider the following practices that support teacher leaders to nurture their self-confidence.

- » **Recognizing their strengths:** Nothing can improve teacher leaders' self-confidence better than taking the time to write a list of their strengths. Though this might be an uncomfortable exercise for some, it's important to try. Also encourage teachers to think beyond their role as educators— everything counts. The point is to name what they are good at so they can take pride in those strengths.

» **Celebrating small wins:** Some teachers feel shy about celebrating themselves, but acknowledging both big and small wins is important. So many accomplishments happen in school that go unnoticed. For example, perhaps a teacher's students mastered a particular essential standard, a teacher's department cut its discipline referrals in half, or a teacher's department won over a challenging parent. The possibilities are endless. The point is: there are many opportunities to celebrate teacher leaders' wins, a practice that boosts confidence over time.

» **Accepting compliments:** Accepting compliments is a great way to grow confidence. Those who aren't accustomed to this might feel shy or embarrassed at first. They might defer, downplay, or return the compliment. This might seem like the humble and noble thing to do, but it actually signals low self-esteem. Teachers experiencing discomfort with compliments can benefit from pausing to reflect on *why*. The best way to become more comfortable receiving compliments is to gracefully accept them with a simple thank-you.

» **Practicing positive thinking:** Constant negative thinking is a confidence killer. Teacher leaders need to make thinking positively a habit. There are plenty of catalysts for negative thinking over the course of the teachers' day—a parent accuses them of being horrible teachers, the teacher leaders make a mistake that affects their team, or the teacher leaders take a risk that doesn't pan out. Whatever the cause of negative thoughts, teacher leaders shouldn't let them squash their budding confidence. Encourage teacher leaders to keep returning to positive thinking to nurture their self-confidence.

» **Avoiding the comparison trap:** Teacher leaders need to be careful to avoid the comparison trap. Comparing oneself to others can be devastating to a person's self-confidence. There will always be teachers in the school who are better at using technology, connecting with a challenging student, or collaborating with parents. However, that doesn't take away from each teacher leader's unique strengths.

» **Setting goals:** Teacher leaders must set goals each year to grow their leadership capacity. This is different from the goal setting teachers do in the classroom. These goals can be about anything that allows teacher leaders to identify an area they want to improve. Certified psychiatric counselor Madhuleena Roy Chowdhury (2019) writes:

By setting goals, we get a road map of where we are heading to and what is the right way that would lead us there. It is a plan that holds us in perspective—the more effectively we make the plan, the better are our chances of achieving what we aim to.

» **Embracing failure:** Strong teacher leaders see failures as opportunities. Failure is inevitable! If teacher leaders practice embracing their mistakes, they can learn from them. It may seem counterintuitive, but over time, this practice boosts a teacher leader's confidence. The alternative is to get defensive, make excuses, or blame others. Nothing good comes out of those responses to failure.

» **Accepting discomfort:** No one likes being uncomfortable, but successful teacher leaders must have the capacity to get out of their comfort zone from time to time. It's common for teacher leaders to stay in their comfort zone because the familiarity of doing things the same way doesn't pose risks. But successful leadership demands that teacher leaders take risks. By making a practice of accepting discomfort as part of the role, teacher leaders will become more confident with time.

» **Increasing competence:** With greater competence comes stronger confidence. Sometimes teacher leaders lack self-confidence because they don't have a thorough understanding of the concept they are implementing. *Competence* means having the specific knowledge and skills to accomplish a task. Increasing competence happens with time, dedication, and practice. Encourage teacher leaders to identify new knowledge and skills they want to develop and then engage with the learning and experiences they need to become experts.

» **Practicing gratitude—and remembering to smile:** Cultivating gratitude is a powerful practice. Feeling and showing appreciation for the positive things in life is a morale booster. And don't forget smiles. Both gratitude and smiles are contagious! The more teacher leaders smile and show appreciation for everything they have, the more this attitude will permeate throughout their department or team. Teacher leaders play a significant role in keeping morale high. A positive and hopeful attitude is a great reflection of a teacher leader's confidence and has a way of inspiring confidence in those who follow them. Consider implementing a *smile challenge* or *gratitude challenge* to help teacher leaders keep all the things they have to smile about top of mind.

Self-confidence is an important leadership skill that leaders must continuously strengthen. They will more successfully influence others when they exude confidence.

The PLC Connection: Collaborative Culture and Collective Responsibility

You know the importance of high-performing teams in a PLC, but sometimes adult drama keeps a team from achieving its full potential. *Adult drama* comes in many forms that can damage the team's ability to collaborate at a high level. Common examples include gossiping, backstabbing, spreading rumors, excluding team members, and exaggerating stories. Whatever the details of the drama, the source is usually some kind of insecurity. When others challenge a person's self-worth, pride, or ego, it's easy to lash out.

How have you seen this play out in your school? Can you see this dynamic at work? Now imagine a team of self-confident teachers. How well do you think this team collaborates? Team members each feel good about themselves, their skill set, and their abilities. Team members each have faith in what they do. Other team members' unique skills don't threaten this team. Instead, the team members embrace everyone's talents because they know collectively, they're stronger.

There are three benefits for having confident collaborative teams advance the PLC work. The first is *more intuitive and empowered decision making*. Leadership coach Ben Brearley (2019) explains, "A confident team will generally need to rely less on their leader to make decisions in their role, and will feel confident that they're on the right track." In other words, confident collaborative teams take ownership of the PLC work without self-doubts and reservations. They know what the right work is for their students and engage in it without needing school administrators to micromanage their efforts.

Second, *confident team members speak up*. Brearley (2019) goes on to write that *confidence* empowers "team members to speak up against bad behavior and also come forward with their ideas more readily. If your team members are staying silent, you're missing opportunities to improve" (Brearley, 2019). If teacher leaders on a collaborative team lack self-confidence, they will never maximize the talents and skills that everyone brings to the table.

Third, *success breeds success*. Every time a team experiences success, it boosts members' self-confidence, and sets them up to experience another success. Journalist Tom Muha (2016) puts it this way: "People's confidence builds as their team's collective effort produces positive outcomes." Imagine a team of self-confident teacher leaders and administrators. Team members each take ownership of every student in their grade level and school, and they are open and honest with one another and share ideas. As a result, the team's student achievement increases. This success also furthers their self-confidence. On the other hand, a team's failures will continue to deteriorate their self-confidence:

> As a team falters, confidence evaporates, and failure feeds on itself as the team tumbles into a doom loop. First, teammates stop talking to one another. In the absence of constructive conversation, a culture of blaming other people for problems begins to evolve. No one wants to be faulted, so team members start avoiding contact with each other. Without teamwork, nothing much gets done, and people lapse into feeling powerless. (Muha, 2016)

Self-confidence is a critical skill teacher leaders must develop to strengthen collaborative teams in a PLC. A high-performing team hinges on the self-confidence of its members.

PAUSE TO REFLECT

Pause for a moment to reflect on the following questions.

» Why is it important for teacher leaders and school leaders to have self-confidence?

» Which practices from the list (see page 50) will best help your leadership team members grow their self-confidence?

» Knowing that self-confidence is an ongoing process, how can you continuously support your leadership team to strengthen it?

» How will developing self-confidence advance the work of your PLC?

Professional Development Activities for Developing Self-Confidence

Now that you've explored the importance of self-confidence and why it's an essential skill of strong teacher leaders, consider professional development activities to help teacher leaders develop self-confidence.

Self-Assessment for Developing Self-Confidence Skills

A self-assessment is a great way for teacher leaders to reflect on their current reality. This tool allows participants to name their strengths and challenges. Figure 4.1 offers a self-assessment teacher leaders can use to determine specific areas they wish to develop.

Instructions: Read each statement and indicate whether it applies to you consistently, usually, occasionally, or rarely. Next, set goals for improving weak aspects of this skill.

	Consistently	Usually	Occasionally	Rarely
Generally, I feel good about myself.	☐	☐	☐	☐
If someone asks me what I'm good at, I can answer easily.	☐	☐	☐	☐
I know I am a valued member of the team.	☐	☐	☐	☐
I don't need praise or reassurances to help me feel better about myself.	☐	☐	☐	☐
I can respectfully speak my mind without fearing how others will react.	☐	☐	☐	☐
I am assertive and can make decisions without worrying about what others will think.	☐	☐	☐	☐
When I make a mistake, I have no problem owning it and apologizing, whether that means apologizing to a student, parent, colleague, or administrator.	☐	☐	☐	☐
I am not afraid to ask for help. I would rather ask for help than be a victim or martyr about everything I have to do.	☐	☐	☐	☐

Look back over your answers. Here, set goals that will support you to improve your self-confidence.

FIGURE 4.1: Assess your self-confidence.

*Visit **go.SolutionTree.com/PLCbooks** for a free reproducible of this figure.*

Conversation Starters

Planned conversation starters are a great way to initiate discussions and allow participants to learn from peers' diverse perspectives.

Use the quotes and discussion questions in figure 4.2 as conversation starters. As a school leadership team, share answers, and participate in a discussion on developing your self-confidence.

Quotes	Discussion Questions
"Don't waste your energy trying to change opinions . . . Do your thing, and don't care if they like it." —Tina Fey	• Think of a time when you tried to change someone's opinion. What happened? • Why do you want others to believe what you believe or see what you see? • Has your opinion ever been in the minority? What did that feel like? • How do you handle it when you are one of the few who feel a certain way about something?
"To overcome fear is the quickest way to gain self-confidence." —Roy T. Bennett	• What are your fears? • How do you think overcoming one of those fears would help you gain more self-confidence? • How does your self-confidence prevent you from overcoming those fears? • What steps can you take to overcome at least one of those fears?
"Be kinder to yourself, and celebrate little wins." —Charlotte Jacklin	• List some wins you had over the last year. • Did you celebrate any of the wins? Why or why not? • What prevents you from celebrating your little wins? • How can you keep a record of all your wins—something you can look back on when you need a self-confidence boost?
"Confidence is contagious. So is lack of confidence." —Vince Lombardi	• How is confidence contagious? • How is lack of confidence contagious? • When did someone's confidence strengthen your self-confidence? • When did someone's lack of confidence impact your self-confidence?
"Confidence comes not from always being right, but from not fearing to be wrong." —Petra McIntyre	• Why do people fear being wrong? • How does not wanting to be wrong impact your jobs as an educator? • How might always needing to be right limit your self-confidence? • How would self-confidence help you to take risks? How would that make you a better educator?

"Whether you think you can, or think you can't—you're right." —Henry Ford	• When have you thought you *could do* something, and why? • When have you thought you *couldn't do* something, and why? • Between thinking that you can and you can't, what do you think more often? • How can you change your way of thinking so you think you *can* more often?
"Confidence is a choice . . . to act, or to do, or to decide." —Katty Kay	• How can you make a choice you will be more confident starting today? • What kinds of things can you do to show you are more confident? • What prevents you from making the choice to be more confident? • Is it important for you to make the choice to be more confident? Why or why not?

FIGURE 4.2: Let's talk about self-confidence conversation starters.

*Visit **go.SolutionTree.com/PLCbooks** for a free reproducible of this figure.*

Case Scenarios

Use any of the following case scenarios to facilitate a discussion with teacher leaders about continuously working to strengthen self-confidence. After reading the case scenario, discuss (1) how having a strong sense of self-confidence will help the colleague in the situation, and (2) how self-confidence will help if you face a similar situation.

CASE SCENARIO ONE

A colleague constantly seeks assurances. When making decisions, she needs someone to tell her the decision is good. When problem solving, she needs someone to tell her the solution she came up with is good. When presenting any change to her department, she needs someone to tell her the change is good. When she does not receive assurances, she doubts everything she is doing. Her colleagues and administrators are getting tired of constantly reassuring her. And if something isn't good, her colleagues and administrators don't want to tell her the truth because they know it will hurt her feelings and fuel her self-doubt.

CASE SCENARIO TWO

One of your colleagues only likes to hear positive feedback or have others stroke his ego. He does not take constructive feedback well. When his administrator provides him with a less-than-exemplary rating on any standard, he gets upset, and resents his administrator. He will obsess over a critique for days and beat himself up, thinking no one appreciates how great he is. He only wants praise and compliments. He is the same with his colleagues. He wants his colleagues to appreciate him and his work, and praise him every time he shares ideas; he does not want to hear that his ideas need more work.

CASE SCENARIO THREE

A colleague has a challenging group of students this year. Every time a student misbehaves, her administrators tell her to call the parents before she writes an office referral. However, she does not like calling the parents because she is afraid of confrontation. It's easier for her not to call the parents, so she just keeps hoping the students will stop misbehaving. Unfortunately, the behavior is getting worse. Finally, when she calls one of the parents, the father yells at her because he had no idea his child was having problems in class. This reinforces the teacher's feelings about not calling parents because she is extremely uncomfortable with that kind of confrontation.

CASE SCENARIO FOUR

One of your colleagues is a people pleaser at heart. He got into education because he likes to serve, has a big heart, and wants to see others do well. Because he is such a people pleaser, he absolutely hates it when people are upset with him. He does not like to see his colleagues, administrators, or teammates mad at him, so he does everything he can to make everyone happy. Many times he does this at the expense of his own happiness and well-being.

CASE SCENARIO FIVE

Others know your colleague for her negative attitude. Nothing makes her happy; she constantly complains about everything. Before and after any staff meeting, she complains about what a waste of time the meeting is. She never praises anyone or anything. She also constantly complains about her students' lack of academic abilities, poor attitude, or inappropriate behavior. She complains about students' parents too, saying they are the reason the students are not doing well in her class. She generally is an unhappy person.

SUBMIT A CASE SCENARIO

Ask teacher leaders to anonymously submit a current scenario that describes someone they know and currently work with (outside the school or district) who lacks self-confidence.

The Agree-or-Disagree Line

Invite participants to examine each of the following statements. Allow participants a few minutes to process, and then ask them to stand on the right side of the room if they agree with the statement or the left side of the room if they disagree with the statement. Once participants have chosen their side, open the floor up for discussion by asking, "Why do you agree or disagree with the statement?" The discussion helps participants learn more about the importance of a teacher leader having self-confidence.

» **Statement one:** To be an effective leader, self-confidence is *the most* important skill.

» **Statement two:** Once you have self-confidence, you are good. It will always be there.

» **Statement three:** Self-confidence is a fixed skill—you either have it or you don't.

» **Statement four:** If you just pretend you are confident, the self-confidence will come.

» **Statement five:** Self-confidence is something that starts when you are a child. As an adult, it is exceedingly difficult to strengthen your self-confidence.

» **Statement six:** Being self-confident makes you a better spouse, parent, teacher, and friend, but you don't know how to reach that level of self-confidence.

» **Statement seven:** I struggle to recognize the line between self-confidence and arrogance.

Journal Prompts

Provide participants with the following prompts and instruct them to choose a few to write about in a journal. This activity is private; you should not expect participants to share their journal. Arrange for participants to revisit this activity after one year. At that time, they should answer the questions again, reflect on the changes in their self-confidence, and notice how those changes have helped them become a better teacher leader.

» What actions and activities make you feel good about yourself?

» What do you do well?

» What can you do to improve the situations that make you feel anxious or nervous?

» In what kinds of situations do you doubt your capabilities?

» Who are the people that improve your life? Who are the people that bring you down?

» What are some things you can do to make yourself proud?

» Who do you know with the same type of confidence you hope to possess? How do you get there?

» What are your three favorite qualities about yourself?

» What kinds of things can you do to boost your confidence?

» For what are you grateful?

Summary

Self-confidence is an important skill for all educators to possess, but it's a non-negotiable quality for teacher leaders. With self-confidence, teacher leaders can do so much more to make themselves stronger leaders. Investing time in your teacher leaders to help them develop their self-confidence will make a significant impact on their ability to lead their colleagues. Consider how your school leadership team can use the activities in this chapter to plan your professional learning about developing self-confidence.

Reflect on Developing Self-Confidence Skills

Pause to reflect on what you've read in this chapter. Use the following prompts to journal about what you learned and next steps you'll take.

Before reading this chapter, how would you have described the relationship between leadership and self-confidence?

After reading this chapter and participating in the activities, what have you learned about your (or your teacher leaders') self-confidence skills?

What do you plan to do to continuously strengthen your (or your teacher leaders') self-confidence skills?

CHAPTER 5

Developing Courageous Skills

Face it—having the courage to have tough conversations is hard for many educators. "Tough conversations are those where you know the other person is not going to be pleased with your message, the message you need to communicate is uncomfortable or awkward, and you know you may hurt the other person's feelings with your message" (Kullar, 2020, p. 59). It's even harder for teacher leaders to have those tough conversations because teachers in their departments or teams are their colleagues. It's so much easier to ignore the tough conversation or hope the issue will just get better on its own than to have the courage to deal with it.

Writer Brittney Maxfield (2019) references a study from the coauthors of *Crucial Conversations*, Joseph Grenny, Kerry Patterson, Ron McMillan, Al Switzler, and Emily Gregory (2022). Grenny and colleagues (2022) find 80 percent of employees procrastinate having those tough conversations. Furthermore, one in four employees puts off having those tough conversations for six months. Respondents were hesitant to have those tough conversations for a variety of reasons, including the following.

» Not having confidence the conversation will go well

» Fearing the consequences of speaking up outweigh the downsides of staying quiet

» Fearing how teammates will react

» Lacking the skill or ability to have the tough conversations

When teacher leaders are hesitant to lead tough conversations, sometimes it's because they believe the conversation itself is unkind. The conversation might make another person upset or angry, so teacher leaders want no part of it, especially when the other person is in their department or team and possibly a friend. This is the reality of teacher leaders' position: they have friendships with their colleagues—those same people they are now in charge of leading. This is the reason teacher leaders need support in developing courage. Having the courage to have tough conversations is difficult for any leader, but even more so for teacher leaders.

In this chapter, I explore tips to help teacher leaders be courageous in having tough conversations. Next, I discuss the PLC connection—specifically to big idea number two (collaborative culture and collective responsibility). The chapter ends with a series of professional development activities to support teacher leaders to develop courage.

Tips for Having Courageous Conversations

As hard as it is to have tough conversations, deep down leaders know hope and avoidance are not strategies. So, if principals want their teams and schools to get better, they must develop courage in their teacher leaders so they can also lead the tough conversations, which are an inevitable part of the school leaders' job. The founder of Leaders Edge, Joanne Trotta (2022), writes, "Courageous leaders see conflict and discomfort as areas that are ripe for transformation and growth. They don't retreat from difficult interactions; they welcome them." Instead of using avoidance or hope, teacher leaders need support and training on how to face the root cause of issues and then handle them directly through tough conversations when needed.

Consider the following tips to help teacher leaders lead tough conversations (Knight, 2015; Kullar, 2020).

» **Change your mindset:** Sometimes it helps *not* to view a tough conversation as a tough conversation. View it as a conversation to make things better in the long run. Maybe it will improve a behavior or the overall team, provide an alternative solution to something, or make a lesson, a presentation, or an email even better if you provide constructive feedback. Change your mindset from having a tough conversation to that of having a conversation to improve the current situation.

» **Know the purpose:** Before having the tough conversation, make sure you know your purpose. *Why* are you having this tough conversation, but more importantly, *what* is it you want to see happen after the conversation? Usually the purpose of a tough conversation is to change behavior, so understand what behavior you want to change and why. Maybe the purpose is to change someone's decision about doing something. Maybe the purpose is giving feedback on a project to improve the project. Whatever the purpose, know and understand why you are having the tough conversation.

» **Be specific:** The tough conversation should be as specific as possible. Clearly state the purpose and ensure everything you say ties back to that purpose. Nothing good comes from bringing up generic statements or past events. Remember your desired outcome for that conversation—you are more likely to reach your goal if you are specific in discussing only the concerns or situation that prompted you to initiate the conversation. If you want something from the person you're talking to, be sure to plainly state what it is you want. Make it clear what you want from the person and ensure you both agree. This will give you the best chance for success.

» **Breathe:** Hope for the best, but prepare for the other person to become defensive, upset, or quiet. It's always possible that the person will not receive a tough conversation well, so it's important to stay in control of your emotions. Breathe and keep the purpose of the conversation top of mind. Remember the outcome you want to see happen after the conversation. Let the other person share emotions; it's natural for people to have complex feelings in response to a tough conversation. Ultimately, though, you should stay in control and focus on the issue.

» **Process your emotions:** No doubt you will be experiencing emotions before you have the conversation as well as during the conversation. Being aware of your emotions should dictate *when* to have that tough conversation. If you are too upset or angry, then it is not the time to engage the other person in dialogue. Wait until you are calm and clear on your intentions, *then* initiate the conversation. This ensures you make the conversation about the issue, instead of making it about you.

» **Take time to prepare:** The more you plan and practice your tough conversation, the better you'll lead it. Preparation is key! Know what you're going to say, when, and how you're going to say it. Know the specifics of the issue, come to the conversation ready to communicate your concern or feedback, and have your request or critique ready. Anticipate the questions and reactions and prepare for them too. If you need to role-play the conversation, do it with someone you trust, maybe another teacher leader or an administrator.

» **Remember that your words matter:** The words you use during difficult conversations matter. The wrong words can cause the other person to get angry, defensive, or defiant. The right words can cause the other person to reflect and change. Wrong words include things like *you always* or *you never, you're unprofessional*, or *you should do this*. Supportive and productive language sounds like "What could we do from here?" "What are we both willing to do to help?" "What is the best solution to resolve this?" "Tell me more about . . ." and "It sounds like . . ."

» **Listen:** Actively listen after you say what you have to say. Inevitably, other people are going to want to share their side; you must let them have their say. Avoid interruptions and getting upset. Just listen. During a tough conversation, listen more than you talk. You opened the dialogue, so it's important the other person feels heard. If you keep interrupting, you may not achieve the intended outcome because the other person never gets to tell you the other side.

» **Be respectful:** Having a tough conversation doesn't mean you have to be rude or condescending. Always be respectful of the person you are having the conversation with. Stick to the facts. Remember your purpose for having that tough conversation. Remain professional. Imagine you are being recorded—How would you want others to hear you? Keep that in mind with your words, tone, and volume.

» **Reflect and learn:** After every tough conversation, reflect and learn. How did the conversation go? Did you meet your purpose of having that conversation? Did you achieve the intended outcome? If the results of the conversation did not go well, it is imperative for you to reflect on what happened. What was said that derailed the conversation? Did you let your emotions get in the way or were you underprepared with the content of the conversation? These things happen, but it's important to learn from every unsuccessful conversation you have; this knowledge will help you get better each time.

The PLC Connection: Collaborative Culture and Collective Responsibility

Courageous skills are critical for high-performing teams. Collaborative meetings bring up many opportunities for courage! Working in a PLC is daunting and demanding. Courage helps team members rise to the occasion and have the tough conversations needed to propel the team forward.

For example, collaborative teams in PLCs tend to have norms that guide their meetings. Some teams will even begin each meeting by reading their norms aloud. Examples of norms include being on time, coming prepared, actively participating, and so on. Creating team norms is a step in the right direction to ensure everyone is prepared for effective and efficient collaboration. But what happens when team members violate the norms? It requires courage to address a norm violation in a PLC.

For collaborative teams to be high performing, team members must openly share their data, such as when a teacher has more students demonstrate mastery on a common assessment. For some teachers, this is difficult—it makes them vulnerable to share that information—so it's tempting to try to get around this expectation. To openly share and look at one another's data in a PLC requires courage.

When teams examine data, they're monitoring progress and looking for ways to improve. They use data to determine how *teachers* are doing; it's a call for self-reflection. Without the courage to examine whether teachers' efforts are succeeding, the focus shifts to students' failures. How many times have you heard a statement like "These are all the kids who are failing, so let's send them to an intervention"? It takes courage to share data, analyze which teachers need to make adjustments, and accept support from colleagues.

During collaboration time, teams make many decisions—decisions about which standards are essential, what the learning target should look like, and which questions to keep or remove from assessments. But what happens if teachers on the collaborative team don't follow through with these decisions when they go back to their classrooms? Teachers in a PLC require the courage to address issues like this; otherwise, they invalidate and undermine the whole collaboration process, eventually leading to dysfunction on the team.

Speaking up respectfully in collaborative meetings is necessary for teams to grow and ensure students receive the best instructional and assessment practices. Imagine a teacher shares an idea about how to reteach a concept or provide enrichment, and another teacher on the team has a different idea, but that teacher stays quiet. That silence does a disservice to everyone on the team, as well as the students. When teachers stay quiet in collaborative meetings and don't offer ideas, suggestions, or constructive criticism, everyone suffers. A PLC culture requires that teacher leaders have the courage to speak up!

Keep in mind, when working as part of a PLC, you are not in the business of keeping others happy, making others feel good, or stroking others' egos. You are in the business of *improving learning for all students*—that is your main purpose. To do this, teams collaborate and use the collective expertise of all members in the team. That requires courage. Doing the right thing always requires courage.

What does it look like when team members develop courage and bring it to their collaboration? Courageous teacher leaders don't hesitate to hold one another accountable for the work—not from a place of shame or control, but with compassion and support. Team members are honest with one another because everyone on the team knows and understands the most important thing is *advancing student learning*. When teacher leaders develop courageous skills and can have tough conversations, everyone shares accountability for keeping their focus on the work. Team members who bring courage to their interactions often avoid adult drama (see page 53) because they do the hard work of holding one another accountable to their PLC's mission.

PAUSE TO REFLECT

Pause for a moment to reflect on the following questions.

» What practices support teacher leaders to successfully engage in tough conversations?

» Why are teacher leaders sometimes hesitant to have tough conversations?

» Why are hope and avoidance not strategies? How will you stop using them as strategies?

» How will developing courageous skills advance the work of your PLC?

Professional Development Activities for Developing Courageous Skills

Now that you've explored the importance of having courageous conversations and why it's essential for strong teacher leaders, consider professional development activities to help teacher leaders develop these skills.

Self-Assessment for Developing Courageous Skills

A self-assessment is a great way for teacher leaders to reflect on their current reality, specifically their strengths and challenges about courage. Provide the self-assessment in figure 5.1 and encourage teacher leaders to determine their specific areas of growth to strengthen this skill.

Instructions: Read each statement and indicate whether it applies to you consistently, usually, occasionally, or rarely. Next, set goals for improving weak aspects of this skill.

	Consistently	Usually	Occasionally	Rarely
I avoid confrontation.	☐	☐	☐	☐
I need people to always be OK with me. When people are upset with me, I have a hard time dealing with it.	☐	☐	☐	☐
I avoid talking to people when I know I need to say something difficult.	☐	☐	☐	☐
Anytime someone else brings up a difficult topic, I change the subject.	☐	☐	☐	☐
I don't always give people my honest opinion because I don't want to hurt anyone's feelings.	☐	☐	☐	☐
I prefer to be passive-aggressive instead of telling people how I feel or what I think.	☐	☐	☐	☐
When I do engage in tough conversations, they never seem to go well. I tend to say things I don't mean to say.	☐	☐	☐	☐

Look back over your answers. Here, set goals that will support you to improve your ability to be courageous in difficult conversations.

FIGURE 5.1: Assess your courage.

*Visit **go.SolutionTree.com/PLCbooks** for a free reproducible of this figure.*

Conversation Starters

Planned conversation starters are a great way to initiate discussions and allow participants to learn from peers' diverse perspectives.

Use the quotes and discussion questions in figure 5.2 as conversation starters. As a school leadership team, share your answers, and participate in a discussion on developing your courage.

Quotes	Discussion Questions
"It's the hard conversations that create good relationships." —Goksi	• How do difficult conversations relate to good relationships? • Have you experienced a tough conversation that improved a relationship? • Think about your strong working relationships. Did having tough conversations help them? • How good would your good relationships be without tough conversations?
"Speak when you are angry and you will make the best speech you will ever regret." —Ambrose Bierce	• How can you prevent yourself from having a tough conversation when you're angry? • What causes you to speak when you're angry? • Think of a time when you regretted what you said during a tough conversation. • What does the author of the quote mean by "speech"? What happens when you get angry in a tough conversation?
"Sometimes the most important conversations are the most difficult to engage in." —Jeanne Phillips	• What makes the most important conversations the most difficult? • Why must these conversations feel so difficult? • What is the difference between an easy conversation and a tough conversation? • What makes a conversation important?
"When we avoid difficult conversations, we trade short-term discomfort for long-term dysfunction." —Peter Bromberg	• What kinds of short-term discomfort happen if you avoid difficult conversations? • Why do you avoid difficult conversations? • What are some examples of long-term dysfunction that happens when you avoid difficult conversations? • How can you commit to having difficult conversations to avoid long-term dysfunction?
"Listening well is one of the most powerful skills you can bring to a difficult conversation." —Douglas Stone	• Why is listening so critical during a tough conversation? • In addition to being critical, why is listening so difficult during a tough conversation? • Share a time when you didn't listen during a tough conversation. How did that conversation turn out? • How can you try to listen more during tough conversations?

"Courage is what it takes to stand up and speak. Courage is also what it takes to sit down and listen." —Winston Churchill	• Why do you need courage to stand up and speak? • What prevents you from having that courage? • Why does it take courage to sit down and listen? • How do you balance having the courage to both speak your mind and also just listen?
"Be brave enough to start a conversation that matters." —Margaret Wheatley	• How do you develop courage to have those tough conversations? • Why do you lack courage to have tough conversations? • How do you decide if a conversation is worth having? • How can you prepare to start a tough conversation?

FIGURE 5.2: Let's talk about courage conversation starters.

*Visit **go.SolutionTree.com/PLCbooks** for a free reproducible of this figure.*

Case Scenarios

Use any of the following case scenarios to facilitate a discussion with teacher leaders about developing courage. After reading the case scenario, discuss how they have that conversation.

CASE SCENARIO ONE

When your team collaborates, members frequently make decisions, like when to give the common formative assessment or how they will grade the assessment. However, there is one teacher on the team who always agrees to the decisions the team makes. But when she goes back to her classroom, this teacher doesn't always follow through. She ends up making her own decisions and says her decisions are in the best interest of the students in her classroom.

CASE SCENARIO TWO

Your collaborative team has created four norms. At every meeting, the team reviews the norms before they begin. One of the norms is to be *attentive*, which includes members staying off cell phones. However, there is one teacher on the team who is constantly on her phone. You haven't addressed this violation of team norms because you don't want to embarrass her; you're hoping she just stops being on her phone, but she still hasn't.

CASE SCENARIO THREE

Your administration announced a decision that involves after-school bus dismissal. You disagree with the new procedure because you think it will cause a lot of chaos.

You prefer the current method of dismissal, which is much more orderly for your grade level. Teachers from your department or team also share the same concern and express it to you.

CASE SCENARIO FOUR

You have a challenging parent who has brought up some valid concerns you addressed in the past. However, he continues to call and email with new concerns. He never seems to be happy with anything you do.

CASE SCENARIO FIVE

You have two teachers in your department or team who are having a hard time getting along. They get along superficially; however, they do not like to share ideas with each other, and they do not value or respect what the other brings to the table. This animosity has been between these two teachers for an exceedingly long time, and other team members have just learned to deal with it.

SUBMIT A CASE SCENARIO

Ask teacher leaders to anonymously submit a current scenario that describes a tough conversation they want to have but haven't yet.

The Agree-or-Disagree Line

Invite participants to examine each of the following statements. Allow participants a few minutes to process the statements, and then ask them to stand on the right side of the room if they agree with the statement or the left side of the room if they disagree with the statement. Once participants have chosen their side, open the floor up for discussion by asking, "Why do you agree or disagree with the statement?" The discussion helps participants learn more about the importance of a teacher leader having the courage to have tough conversations.

> » **Statement one:** I want to keep the peace, and the best way to do that is to avoid tough conversations.

> » **Statement two:** I know I'm a people pleaser. I don't like it when people are upset with me.

> » **Statement three:** It is difficult to hold my emotions back. When I'm upset, I let people know.

> » **Statement four:** I think teachers are professionals and adults; it's not my job to tell them anything different.

» **Statement five:** Despite being a teacher leader, I have no authority to have tough conversations with my colleagues.

» **Statement six:** The hardest part about having a tough conversation is how to start.

» **Statement seven:** When people ask me for my opinions, I'm never honest. I always say things like "that looks great" or "great idea."

Activity for Developing Courageous Skills

A great way to practice having tough conversations is through role playing. Pair teacher leaders and have one partner volunteer to play the role of the teacher, while the other is the teacher leader. Then have them switch roles. At the end of each role-play scenario (or after both participants have played both roles), have the pairs reflect on their conversations. What went well and what mistakes were made in the dialogue? The purpose is for teacher leaders to get practice leading tough conversations with the teachers in their department or team.

ROLE-PLAYING SCENARIO ONE

Teacher A (playing a teacher): Act out being extremely negative about everything. Teaching has become really hard, the students are challenging, and there is no support from administrators.

Teacher B (playing the teacher leader): Lead a tough conversation with Teacher A.

ROLE-PLAYING SCENARIO TWO

Teacher A (playing a teacher): Act out not being happy about a new change being rolled out specifically related to your PLC. The change is that all teachers now must share students during interventions. This teacher does not want to; she wants to keep her own students.

Teacher B (playing the teacher leader): Lead a tough conversation with Teacher A.

ROLE-PLAYING SCENARIO THREE

Teacher A (playing a teacher): Act out not liking a particular student. Complain about how awful this student is and that there is nothing you can do for him.

Teacher B (playing the teacher leader): Lead a tough conversation with Teacher A.

ROLE-PLAYING SCENARIO FOUR

Teacher A (playing a teacher): Act out not liking administrators. Talk about how you think they are unsupportive and how none of their decisions make sense.

Teacher B (playing the teacher leader): Lead a tough conversation with Teacher A.

ROLE-PLAYING SCENARIO FIVE

Teacher A (playing a teacher): Act out going through a really tough time at home, which is causing you to come to school late and always ask your teammates to cover your morning duty station, along with other things.

Teacher B (playing the teacher leader): Lead a tough conversation with Teacher A.

ROLE-PLAYING SCENARIO SIX

Teacher A (playing a teacher): Act out liking the status quo. If there is a choice between doing something the same way you have for years and changing, you pick the former. You turned out fine, so why can't you teach the same way you were taught? Why does anything need to change?

Teacher B (playing the teacher leader): Lead a tough conversation with Teacher A.

Summary

Having the courage to lead tough conversations is a big part of any leader's job, including teacher leaders'. Avoiding having the conversations or hoping the issues will just resolve themselves on their own is not effective leadership. Teacher leaders owe it to students to have those tough conversations when needed. Teacher leaders should be respectful, prepare for the tough conversation, and remember the larger purpose of furthering the work of the PLC. Consider how your school leadership team can use the activities in this chapter to plan your professional learning about developing courage.

Reflect on Developing Courageous Skills

Pause to reflect on what you've read in this chapter. Use the following prompts to journal about what you learned and next steps you'll take.

Before reading this chapter, how would you have described the relationship between leadership and having courage?

After reading this chapter and participating in the activities, what have you learned about your (or your teacher leaders') courageous skills?

What do you plan to do to continuously strengthen your (or your teacher leaders') courageous skills?

CHAPTER 6

Developing Conflict-Resolution Skills

nevitably, educators will encounter conflict. All educators would love to work in a team where there are no disagreements, and everyone just magically agrees with everything all the time. It's a place where there are no hurt feelings or bruised egos; no feelings of frustration or anger; and no insults or mean comments. But of course, you know that's not real life. Conflict will occur and how a leader navigates that conflict is critical to the success of the team.

In their study, professors and researchers Benjamin Laker and Vijay Pereira (2022) find the number one thing new leaders worry about most is "dealing with conflict on my team." The coauthors stress the importance of leaders learning how to resolve conflicts and state that "managing conflict is a skill, and one that many leaders are never taught. When it's not handled well, conflict can wreak havoc on your team" (Laker & Pereira, 2022).

Conflict is not always a bad thing. In fact, teams and schools need healthy conflict to grow. *Healthy conflicts* are productive disagreements that result in meaningful change. Healthy conflicts allow people to be honest about their perspective while still being respectful. A hallmark of healthy conflict is it focuses on the issue itself rather than on any one individual. An example of a healthy conflict is when one teacher engages another about conflicting grading philosophies. In the healthy conflict, both teachers express their views professionally while hearing each other out and seeking a mutually beneficial solution. Consider the following reasons healthy conflict may benefit educators (Sharma, 2023).

1. **Boosts security and trust:** People feel more secure when they handle conflict well, which also results in building trust among team members.

2. **Helps people value diverse perspectives:** Healthy conflict allows people to openly speak up and share their opinions without fear.

3. **Supports better decision-making skills:** With everyone openly sharing their perspectives, the team is able to come up with better solutions.

4. **Acts as a preventive measure:** When healthy conflict occurs as soon as issues arise, it prevents that conflict from building into a much bigger conflict, which then is harder to resolve.

5. **Builds team bonds:** Healthy conflict strengthens the bond between teammates.

As beneficial as healthy conflict is for a team, unhealthy conflict is not. *Unhealthy conflicts* can become personal. When that happens, colleagues can become defensive, which usually sabotages team productivity. Other times unhealthy conflict is saying nothing at all and just avoiding the issues altogether. Workplace conflict coach Natalie Garramone (2020) writes, "Unhealthy conflict often involves denial of the existence of problems, avoidance of dealing with issues, anger, blame, and manipulation. In unhealthy conflict, there are no real winners." In a grading conflict, imagine instead of talking about their differences, the two teachers stay silent and continue doing what they've always done. How might that play out? Imagine they do speak up about their differences, but the conversation turns into personal attacks. What outcome might that conversation produce? Notice that in both cases, teachers will likely lose connection and sabotage productivity.

It's tempting to think conflict is always bad, but that's not the case. Educators should practice evaluating whether conflicts are healthy or unhealthy and respond accordingly.

Effectively managing conflict (or preventing a healthy conflict from becoming an unhealthy one) requires a proactive approach. Consider the following tips for ensuring a conflict remains healthy (Grady, 2016).

1. **Be assertive:** *Being assertive* means communicating clearly what you want and need from your team without putting anyone down, and without keeping your wants and needs to yourself.

2. **Get to the point:** Being vague or avoiding the real topic leads to confusion. Say what you need to say respectfully.

3. **Pay attention to behavior:** Look at how people are receiving your message. Pick up cues when people may not be hearing what you are saying and adjust accordingly.

4. **Replace *you* language with *I* language:** By speaking using *I* instead of *you*, you will decrease the chances of your team taking the message personally, and therefore, they'll be less likely to be defensive. So instead of saying "you should" or "you always," replace it with "I feel" or "I need."

5. **Focus on the issue, not the person:** Another way to decrease defensiveness is to focus on the issue. Ask, "What is the problem you want to discuss?" instead of making it about a person in your team. Instead of saying, "You didn't bring the data to our team meeting," say "We really need the data at our team meeting, so what can we do to make that happen?"

6. **Paraphrase:** When someone else on your team is sharing something that could result in a conflict, paraphrase what the person said to ensure you understand the message. When people feel they have been heard, it decreases the chances of a conflict becoming unhealthy.

7. **Seek understanding, not agreement:** Make an effort to understand the other person's viewpoint, instead of trying to convince the person to agree with your viewpoint.

Having strong conflict-resolution skills is important for teacher leaders. A report finds over 85 percent of employees in all sectors have experienced conflict to some degree. If the leader does not effectively resolve the conflict, it can lead to a negative impact on the organization's effectiveness, productivity, and morale (CPP, 2008).

Knowing and understanding how to resolve conflicts is essential to your team's work. Consider the following tips for supporting teacher leaders to develop and strengthen conflict-resolution skills (Amaresan, 2023).

» Don't point fingers.

» Let the person explain and actively listen.

» Show a willingness to compromise or collaborate.

» Don't talk behind people's backs.

» Don't take anything personally.

» Pay close attention to nonverbal communication.

» Prioritize resolving the conflict over being "right."

» Know when to apologize and forgive.

» Focus on the conflict at hand, not past conflicts.

» Remember the importance of the relationship.

In this chapter, I explore practices to help teacher leaders successfully mediate conflict. Next, I discuss the PLC connection—specifically to big idea number two (collaborative culture and collective responsibility). The chapter ends with a series of professional development activities to support teacher leaders to develop conflict-resolution skills.

Practices for Mediating Conflict

When conflict occurs in a PLC, leaders should step in and mediate to resolve it. Mediating conflicts is not easy, so hopefully the following tips will help teach teacher leaders who mediate a conflict in their team (Andreev, 2023).

» **Be calm and establish dialogue:** First and foremost, you (as the teacher leader) must engage the teachers in conflict in a dialogue. If no one is talking, or the teachers are avoiding having to talk about the conflict, then that conflict is only going to get worse with time. Think of this as a challenge you want to overcome. Engage the teachers in dialogue so they can at least begin the process of reaching a resolution. No matter what is said during that conversation, it is imperative that as the leader, you remain calm.

» **Remain neutral:** While the dialogue is taking place, you must ensure you do not take sides. Even if you know someone is right, you must remain neutral. Showing any kind of favoritism will make the conflict worse. Ask questions and keep the conversation going until the teachers in your team reach a resolution on their own.

» **Investigate the root issue:** This is a difficult part of mediating a conflict in your team. Sometimes the teachers in the conflict may not even realize what the source of the conflict is; usually, it is because the conflict has been left unresolved for so long. It's important to get to the source so the teachers can truly resolve the conflict.

» **Talk to each side:** Sometimes it helps to have individual, one-to-one conversations with each person to gain perspective on the issues. It also helps the teachers open up to you individually first before getting into a room altogether. This is also a good time to find out how the teachers want to resolve the conflict.

» **Identify potential solutions:** Ideally, you want to find a solution that all parties agree to. Sometimes it can be as simple as an apology and an awareness of not doing something again, but other times it might need to be a specific action plan. Either way, the parties must discuss and agree to a solution or an action plan to help resolve the conflict and move on.

» **Follow up:** After the mediation, it is important to follow up with all parties to see how they implemented the action steps or agreed-on decisions. This follow-up is a necessary part of the conflict-resolution process because it is the only way to check if the teachers have resolved the conflict.

As you review these tips and strategies to help strengthen teacher leaders' conflict-resolution skills, it's also important to understand the role *personality* plays in resolving conflict. Coauthors Kenneth Thomas and Ralph Kilmann's Thomas-Kilmann Instrument highlights five conflict-resolution styles (Kilmann Diagnostics, n.d.).

1. **Collaborating:** Sees conflict as a problem that needs a solution and looks for a solution that will satisfy all parties
    a. *Pros* — Builds trust and relationships while identifying high-quality solutions
    b. *Cons* — Is time-consuming
    c. *When to use* — Enough time and everyone is committed to resolving the conflict

2. **Avoiding:** Sees conflict as something to avoid; finds it easier to withdraw from a conflict instead of facing it
    a. *Pros* — Won't escalate the conflict and keeps the peace
    b. *Cons* — Unresolved conflict can lead to bigger issues
    c. *When to use* — The issue is trivial and does not really matter

3. **Competing:** Sees conflict as a way to win the argument; overpowers teammates to accept the individual's solutions or ideas; getting the individual's way is more important than the relationship
    a. *Pros* — Resolves the conflict quickly
    b. *Cons* — Possibly damages trust and relationships
    c. *When to use* — Quick turnaround time or quick action needed

4. **Accommodating:** Sees conflict as a way to give others what they want; wants others to like the individual, so does whatever needs to be done to prevent any damage to the relationships

    a. *Pros* — Maintains relationships

    b. *Cons* — Possibly leads to resentment

    c. *When to use* — Issue doesn't mean as much to the individual as it does to others

5. **Compromising:** Sees conflict as a way to give up a part of what the individual wants while persuading others to do the same; is all about reaching middle ground

    a. *Pros* — Maintains relationships

    b. *Cons* — May not produce the best solution

    c. *When to use* — Can live with the consequences

Figure 6.1 provides a tool for considering your conflict-resolution style.

Indicate which conflict-resolution style you use the most in the following situations.						
	With your significant other?	With your children?	With your parents?	With your friends?	With your colleagues?	With your supervisor?
Collaborating	☐	☐	☐	☐	☐	☐
Avoiding	☐	☐	☐	☐	☐	☐
Competing	☐	☐	☐	☐	☐	☐
Accommodating	☐	☐	☐	☐	☐	☐
Compromising	☐	☐	☐	☐	☐	☐

Source: Adapted from Kilmann Diagnostics, n.d.

FIGURE 6.1: TKI assessment tool.

Knowing their conflict-resolution style can help teacher leaders identify their strengths and challenges with this skill, as well as set goals for growth. In the next section, I take a closer look at how conflict resolution supports teacher leaders to carry out the work of their PLC.

The PLC Connection: Collaborative Culture and Collective Responsibility

Richard DuFour (n.d.) discusses the concept of an "education lottery" in a Global PD Teams video clip titled *Effective Leaders Don't Leave Learning to Chance*. In this video, DuFour (n.d.) shares how a student's educational experience is very dependent on the *luck of the draw* (or which teacher the student is assigned). Some teachers take points off for late work, others do not; some teachers give bonus points for extra work, others do not; some teachers provide opportunities for retakes, others do not. All of this variability leads to an education lottery for students; their grade is not about what they learned, but rather, more about the grading philosophies and practices of the teacher! So as you work toward becoming a PLC, addressing these different grading practices is critical. However, many times educators avoid this discussion because they want to avoid the likely conflict.

The reality is, conflict is inevitable for educators working in collaborative teams. As your team is prioritizing standards, maybe someone on the team doesn't agree with what others think should be priority standards. Or maybe someone wants a specific question on a common assessment, but another person on the team does not. Conflict on a team often arises about grading—for example, when the team is trying to come to a consensus about general grading practices or how to grade a specific assessment.

Conflict will also likely occur when teams review data to make decisions about interventions and how they will reteach concepts. Educators sometimes avoid these conversations because of a fear of conflict. The purpose of data is to discuss what teachers did or did not do well—not necessarily the students. And when discussing what the teachers did or did not do well, the next conversation is about what the teachers will do differently during the reteaching intervention. You don't want teachers reteaching the same way because it didn't work the first time—however, having that conversation could result in conflict.

From these examples, you can see how growing conflict-resolution skills supports teacher leaders in a PLC. School leaders must have deliberate and productive conversations to resolve conflicts that inevitably arise in collaborative teams. The professional learning activities I outline in the next section are designed to help teacher leaders grow their conflict-resolution skills.

PAUSE TO REFLECT

Pause for a moment to reflect on the following questions.

» What are some of the reasons teacher leaders encounter conflict in their role?

» How can you encourage healthy conflict? How can you discourage unhealthy conflict?

» What strategy will you implement to support teacher leaders on your campus to resolve conflicts?

» How will developing conflict-resolution skills advance the work of your PLC?

Professional Development Activities for Developing Conflict-Resolution Skills

Now that you've explored the importance of managing conflict well and why it's an essential skill of strong teacher leaders, consider professional development activities to help teacher leaders develop conflict-resolution skills.

Self-Assessment for Developing Conflict-Resolution Skills

A self-assessment is a great way for teacher leaders to reflect on their current reality, specifically their strengths and challenges about resolving conflict. Provide teacher leaders the self-assessment in figure 6.2 and encourage them to determine specific areas of growth to strengthen conflict-resolution skills.

Instructions: Read each statement and indicate whether it applies to you consistently, usually, occasionally, or rarely. Next, set goals for improving weak aspects of this skill.	Consistently	Usually	Occasionally	Rarely
I take things personally, which sometimes can lead to conflict.	☐	☐	☐	☐
It's difficult for me to take constructive criticism from others, which can sometimes lead to conflict.	☐	☐	☐	☐
It's hard for me to stay calm when I'm in a conflict.	☐	☐	☐	☐

It's difficult for me to let go of past conflicts.	☐	☐	☐	☐
I have a need to be "right," which can lead to conflict.	☐	☐	☐	☐
I have no issue compromising to resolve conflicts.	☐	☐	☐	☐
I'm a people pleaser, so I avoid conflict at all costs.	☐	☐	☐	☐
Avoiding conflicts does help because relationships don't get ruined.	☐	☐	☐	☐
Look back over your answers. Here, set goals that will support you to improve your ability to resolve conflict.				

FIGURE 6.2: Assess your conflict-resolution skills.

*Visit **go.SolutionTree.com/PLCbooks** for a free reproducible of this figure.*

Conversation Starters

Planned conversation starters are a great way to initiate discussions about conflict resolution and allow participants to learn from their peers' diverse perspectives.

Use the quotes and discussion questions in figure 6.3 as conversation starters. As a school leadership team, share your answers, and participate in a discussion about developing your conflict-resolution skills.

Quotes	Discussion Questions
"Conflict is inevitable but combat is optional." —Max Lucado	• What is the difference between conflict and combat? • Why is conflict inevitable? • How can conflict turn into combat? • How do you prevent turning conflict into combat?

FIGURE 6.3: Let's talk about conflict resolution conversation starters. continued ▶

Quotes	Discussion Questions
"Arguments drag out because one is too stubborn to forgive and the other is too proud to apologize." —Unknown	• What are some reasons people drag out conflicts? • Why is it difficult to forgive people? • What are some ways you can forgive people? What are some ways you can help others in your team forgive people? • How does pride impact the ability to apologize?
"All conflict can be traced back to someone's feelings getting hurt." —Liane Moriarty	• What do feelings have to do with conflict? • How can you consider a colleague's feelings as you navigate conflict? • What do you think started the conflict? • Why is it important to know the origin of a conflict?
"An eye for an eye will only make the whole world blind." —Mahatma Gandhi	• How does the concept "an eye for an eye" relate to conflict? • Is letting conflicts go a good thing? Why or why not? • Why do some conflicts drag on? • How long do you let a conflict go on? How and when is it time to resolve the conflict?
"Knowing when to fight is just as important as knowing how." —Terry Goodkind	• What are some reasons you should engage in conflict? • How do you know whether getting into a conflict is a good idea? • In what situations do you decide not to get into a conflict? • Once you decide to get into a conflict, how do you prepare?
"If you avoid conflict to keep the peace, you start a war inside yourself." —Cheryl Richardson	• What "wars" do you wage with yourself when you avoid conflict? • Describe a time when you were "at war" with yourself because you avoided a conflict? • How does addressing conflict affect you differently than avoiding it? • Knowing the negative impact that avoidance has, why do people still avoid conflict?
"An apology is the superglue of life. It can repair just about anything." —Lynn Johnston	• Do you agree that an apology can "repair just about anything"? Why or why not? • Why is it sometimes so difficult to apologize? • What is the difference between a genuine and a disingenuous apology? • How do you encourage others to admit when they are wrong and offer an apology?

*Visit **go.SolutionTree.com/PLCbooks** for a free reproducible of this figure.*

Case Scenarios

Use any of the following case scenarios to facilitate a discussion with teacher leaders about the importance of developing conflict-resolution skills. After reading the case scenario, ask participants to share how they would resolve conflict in the situation.

CASE SCENARIO ONE

A teacher in your team is really upset that you became the teacher leader for the team. She feels she should have been in that role. You know she's upset because she has been behaving differently toward you. She has told multiple people on the team that she does not think you are the right person to lead the team. She has been trying to get an administrator job and feels that being in this teacher leader role would help her. Her anger toward you makes it difficult because every time you have a team meeting, she does not participate and can be very passive-aggressive.

CASE SCENARIO TWO

A teacher in your department has come to you for help. He is struggling with a parent who has been exceedingly difficult to speak to. The teacher feels he can't do anything right with this parent. No matter what happens, the parent calls him out, sends heated emails, or leaves angry voicemails. When this teacher speaks to the parent or emails him back, it never resolves anything; in fact, it tends to make the situation worse! The conflict between the teacher and the parent has really taken a toll on this teacher. He is rethinking staying in education because he does not feel the parents respect him as a teacher.

CASE SCENARIO THREE

You are upset with an administrator. Some personality issues in your team keep you going to her for help, but she has not provided any support or guidance on how to resolve the issues in your team. You feel like you are doing this job on your own. As a result, you are getting more and more frustrated with your administrator, but your administrator has no idea how you feel.

CASE SCENARIO FOUR

There is a new teacher in your team with many ideas—all of which will involve changing a lot of the ways teachers have done things for several years. She is coming on extraordinarily strong with her opinions, thinks she is "right," and received the job for this very reason. She has turned off others in the team by making members feel they have been doing things "wrong." The team believes this new teacher and teammate is there to tell the other members how to do their job. They resent the new teacher for making them feel this way.

You have lots of different personalities in your team and those differences tend to cause a lot of conflict. For example, one team member is very laid-back and rarely approaches anything with a sense of urgency. Others feel he is lazy and does not care. There is another member of the team who has many ideas and is always wanting to do more. Others feel she needs to "calm down." There is another member who thinks he is smarter than everyone else in the team. Others in the team feel he can be condescending at times. However, on the surface, the team looks fine as members are all cordial with one another. But all these different personalities create unresolved conflict, and as a result, the team is not functioning the way it should.

Ask teacher leaders to anonymously submit a current scenario that describes a conflict.

The Agree-or-Disagree Line

Invite participants to examine each of the following statements. Allow participants a few minutes to process, and then ask them to stand on the right side of the room if they agree with the statement or the left side of the room if they disagree with the statement. Once participants have chosen their side, open the floor up for discussion by asking, "Why do you agree or disagree with the statement?" The discussion will help participants learn more about the importance of a teacher leader having conflict-resolution skills.

» **Statement one:** Resolving conflicts is always difficult.

» **Statement two:** I prefer to avoid conflict.

» **Statement three:** I don't mind conflict because I get passionate about doing what I think is right.

» **Statement four:** If you ignore the conflict for a while, it tends to go away.

» **Statement five:** Conflict and self-confidence are related. The higher your confidence levels, the stronger your conflict-resolution skills.

» **Statement six:** Conflicts are always resolved if people just apologize to one another.

» **Statement seven:** I struggle to know when to step in to resolve a conflict and when to let others resolve it.

Activity for Developing Conflict-Resolution Skills

Provide one index card and a pen to each teacher leader. Ask participants each to write on the index card four words they think of when they hear the word *conflict*. Example words include *fight, jealousy, misunderstanding, awkward,* and *tension*. Once all the participants have their four words, pair the teacher leaders (McGroarty, 2022).

Instruct partners to review their eight words and decide which four best associate with the word *conflict*. Once the pairs decide their four, have them write those on the other side of the index card.

As you debrief, have teacher leaders answer these questions:

- Was there conflict during the "negotiations"?
- How did you feel about this activity?
- Did anyone try to harness control of the situation?
- Looking back, would you do anything differently?
- What techniques helped you decide on the four words?
- Did you learn anything from this exercise? (McGroarty, 2022)

I added the following two questions to McGroarty's (2022) list.

- » How can you use the activity strategies more frequently?
- » What prevents you from using this strategy in other situations?

Summary

Conflict-resolution skills are worth strengthening because conflict is inevitable for collaborative teams in a PLC. Successfully answering the four critical questions of a PLC requires teams to navigate conflict well. Whether it is about standards, assessments or grading, or providing interventions and enrichment, conflict will occur. And as conflicts come up, it is important to embrace the healthy conflicts, but have the skills to resolve the unhealthy conflicts. Resolving conflicts will lead to a more effective team where trust, transparency, and open and honest dialogue occur without fear. How you navigate and successfully resolve those conflicts will predict the successful outcome of your team's work for your students. Consider how your school leadership team can use the activities in this chapter to plan your professional learning about developing conflict-resolution skills.

REPRODUCIBLE

Reflect on Developing Conflict-Resolution Skills

Pause to reflect on what you've read in this chapter. Use the following prompts to journal about what you learned and next steps you'll take.

Before reading this chapter, how would you have described the relationship between leadership and conflict resolution?

After reading this chapter and participating in the activities, what have you learned about your (or your teacher leaders') conflict-resolution skills?

What do you plan to do to continuously strengthen your (or your teacher leaders') conflict-resolution skills?

CHAPTER 7

Developing Lifelong-Learning Skills

*L*ifelong learning is a skill people often admire in leaders. What does this term actually mean? "Lifelong Learning is an approach to learning—whether in personal or professional contexts—that is continuous and self-motivated. Lifelong Learning can be formal or informal, and takes place throughout an individual's life, 'from cradle to grave'" (Nichols, n.d.). Teacher leaders should not only engage in lifelong learning for their own growth as leaders but also model its importance to their colleagues and students.

The key to lifelong learning is that it's "continuous and self-motivated" (Nichols, n.d.). This means even after earning an advanced degree, learning continues. Even after earning a certificate, learning continues. Even after attending a conference, learning continues. In addition, lifelong learning is *self-motivated*, which means no one is telling you to learn something. You are doing it on your own because you have an innate drive and desire to be better both in your personal and professional life.

In this chapter, I explore practices to help teacher leaders commit to becoming lifelong learners. Next, I discuss the PLC connection—specifically to big idea number three (a results orientation). The chapter ends with a series of professional development activities to support teacher leaders to become lifelong learners.

Practices for Becoming a Lifelong Learner

The world is changing rapidly, thanks to technological advancements. In fact, speaker and author on education and workforce development Brandon Busteed (2020) states, "We are now closer to the year 2050 than the year 1990. Let that sink in for a bit." Think about that. How many of you vividly remember the 1990s? They're actually way more in the past when compared to what's coming in the future. So what does that have to do with lifelong learning?

With the rise of the internet, new information is available at unprecedented rates. And now with the mass availability of generative artificial intelligence (AI) technology, the rate of information will only continue to increase:

> With the rapid advance of technologies, being constantly studying is a necessity. New discoveries are appearing, new products and reflections are being made about society, and everything you learned in school years ago isn't enough to keep up with the changes. (SYDLE, 2023)

Therefore, educators should continue to learn well past college graduation to stay current. Lifelong learning has become a necessary skill, including for teacher leaders. Lifelong learners and coauthors Nancy Merz Nordstrom and Jon F. Merz (2006) identify ten reasons why lifelong learning is so important.

1. Leads to an enriching life of self-fulfillment
2. Helps you make new friends and establish valuable relationships
3. Keeps you involved as an active contributor to society
4. Helps you find meaning in your life
5. Helps you adapt to change
6. Makes the world a better place
7. Increases your wisdom
8. Creates a curious, hungry mind
9. Opens your mind
10. Helps you fully develop your natural abilities

What prevents teacher leaders from being lifelong learners? *Time*, for one thing. However, seeing the importance and value of lifelong learning, educators must prioritize the tasks they perform on a daily basis and fit learning into their schedules. Think about the areas where you waste time—scrolling social media, watching TV, or playing video games—and replace some with active learning. Or pair learning with an activity, such as walking and listening to a podcast on a topic you want to learn more about. Make lifelong learning a priority and fit it into your schedule because learning should be a constant in your life as you continue to get better.

Sometimes it's about the old saying, "Ignorance is bliss." Educators are essentially afraid to engage in lifelong learning because once they know something, they must change something. So it's easier to just be ignorant and not learn anything because that allows you to continue to do what you're doing (or maintain the status quo). But think about your profession—education—it's about learning! The day you stop valuing the importance of learning is the day you should rethink being an educator.

Consider the following practices for embracing lifelong learning.

» **Join an association:** There are so many associations in education you can join, but the benefit of those memberships is the access you will get to materials, webinars, workshops, and conferences. In addition, joining an association is a great way to network with other educators, so you can learn from one another. Think about being a member of a group that specializes in your subject area. You'll gain access to all the latest research, tips, and strategies for teaching that content area.

» **Don't forget about soft skills:** Learning isn't always about the *hard skills* (or technical skills) you need to be an educator. Learning can also be about *soft skills* (like emotional intelligence, interpersonal relationships, creativity, and so on) as well. In fact, the soft skills in this book are equally important to gain to become a better leader and educator. Think about lifelong learning in terms of the characteristics that will support your personal and professional growth.

» **Set goals:** Teachers are no strangers to setting goals. However, they're not always practiced at setting goals in the area of continued learning. What area do you want to learn more about and how will you demonstrate you learned it? For example, if you decide you, as a leader, want to learn to react less to stress, create a plan for how you will do that. What resources will you rely on and how will you monitor growth? Or you might decide you want to learn more about a specific districtwide initiative. Again, create a plan for what resources you will use and how you will monitor your learning.

» **Create a resource library:** Create a library of resources not just for yourself but also for your team. If time is an obstacle for lifelong learning, be the resource provider for yourself and others by having access to various articles, videos, books, and so on, and arrange them by topic. Every time you read an article or review a website you learned something from, put it in your library. This library can be a shared drive of resources or maybe even a physical area in your classroom or office.

» **Share what you learn:** Engage other teacher leaders in lifelong learning debriefs, where you discuss your new learning. Create a forum outside your leadership team meetings to just discuss and reflect on your new knowledge. These could be quick chats you set time aside for—maybe during lunch or before school once a month. The purpose is twofold: (1) to get an accountability partner (you and your partner hold each other accountable for learning) and (2) to share your learning with each other so you can continue to grow.

» **Find your learning style:** Learning doesn't always have to be through reading a long textbook on pedagogy and theories. Make learning relevant and engaging by using the medium you find most effective for your learning style. For some, it could be through reading short articles or social media platforms. For others, it could be watching videos. And yet for others, it could be listening to podcasts. Learning can happen through many different platforms, which makes lifelong learning much more accessible.

» **Challenge yourself and your colleagues:** Look at the company you keep. The people you spend a lot of time around should help lift you up. You grow each day to become a better educator and a better leader because your teammates push you to be better. They won't let you become stale.

» **Seek feedback:** Actively solicit feedback from stakeholders (students, teachers, and parents) through surveys or one-on-one conversations. Keep an open mind and seek to discover your strengths and areas for growth.

Teachers appointed to leadership positions are most likely qualified, but their learning doesn't stop. Lifelong learning is critical for school leaders to continue to grow and learn so they can be the best leaders they can be for their students and school community.

The PLC Connection: A Results Orientation

PLCs are deeply rooted in the lifelong learning concept. The definition of a *PLC* begins with the word *ongoing* (DuFour et al., 2024), which means there will never be a day when you arrive at school and your work is done. Even once a school becomes a Model PLC school, the work is still ongoing, and therefore lifelong. However, now your work itself ties to your learning. As teachers collaborate about the four critical questions of a PLC, they are continuously learning from one another.

One way this shows up in PLC work is in examining student assessment data. Team discussions focus on which practices worked and didn't work. This involves an honest reflection from each teacher and a willingness to keep an open mind about learning a different way to teach. Reteaching should not be teaching content the same way the team taught it the first time—*reteaching* means teaching it a different way since the first time didn't work. This requires learning a new or different way to teach.

Sometimes learning may not be about instructional practices; maybe it's about assessment practices. When reviewing the data, the team could realize the assessment itself is flawed and didn't capture what the students learned. This type of honest reflection also involves teachers keeping an open mind about rewriting assessments, which means they may need to learn about different assessment practices since the one they currently use didn't work.

While analyzing and reviewing data, teachers may realize they are using practices in their classroom that don't fully support students (for example, taking twenty minutes of a forty-five-minute class to review a warm-up, using rubrics to grade neatness and effort on projects instead of students' understanding of the standards, or only recognizing students who earn As on tests). Honest reflection requires teachers to keep an open mind about their current practices, how long they've used them, and whether it's time to try something different.

Lifelong learning is deeply rooted in the PLC process, which we've already established in this section as an ongoing process. Being part of a PLC is all about continuously learning from colleagues, growing as professionals, and making changes when needed based on students' learning. This work is all based on results, not effort. It's not about how hard teachers work, but if teachers produce results. And if the results of learning are not there, then learning must occur to determine what needs to happen to ensure the desired results. Because lifelong learning is essential to PLC culture, all leaders must examine ways they can develop the skill.

PAUSE TO REFLECT

Pause for a moment to reflect on the following questions.

» Why is it important for teacher leaders to commit to lifelong learning?

» What obstacles keep teacher leaders from becoming lifelong learners? How can they overcome these obstacles?

» What is the opposite of being a lifelong learner? Why would teacher leaders want to avoid that? How might they avoid that?

» How will developing lifelong learning advance the work of your PLC?

Professional Development Activities for Developing Lifelong-Learning Skills

Now that you've explored the importance of developing lifelong learning and why it's an essential skill of strong teacher leaders, consider professional development activities to help teacher leaders develop the skill of lifelong learning.

Self-Assessment for Developing Lifelong-Learning Skills

A self-assessment is a great way for teacher leaders to reflect on their current reality, specifically their strengths and challenges. Provide teacher leaders the self-assessment in figure 7.1 and encourage them to determine specific areas of growth to strengthen the skill of lifelong learning.

Instructions: Read each statement and indicate whether it applies to you consistently, usually, occasionally, or rarely. Next, set goals for improving weak aspects of this skill.

	Consistently	Usually	Occasionally	Rarely
I enjoy reading professional articles and books.	☐	☐	☐	☐
When I attend professional conferences, I'm inspired to come back and implement my new learning.	☐	☐	☐	☐
Learning new things inspires me to do things differently.	☐	☐	☐	☐

I make changes to my teaching and leadership practices because of what I learn.	☐	☐	☐	☐
My experiences have taught me everything I need to know about being a teacher.	☐	☐	☐	☐
I learn new things, but I don't like to make changes because what I do works.	☐	☐	☐	☐
I understand the value of learning, but I feel like educational practices and philosophies just recycle over time.	☐	☐	☐	☐
Learning can be difficult because it challenges all the things I know work and all the things I'm comfortable doing.	☐	☐	☐	☐

Look back over your answers. Here, set goals that will support you to improve your ability to be a lifelong learner.

FIGURE 7.1: Assess your lifelong-learning skills.

*Visit **go.SolutionTree.com/PLCbooks** for a free reproducible of this figure.*

Conversation Starters

Planned conversation starters are a great way to initiate discussions about lifelong learning and allow participants to learn from peers' diverse perspectives.

Use the quotes and discussion questions in figure 7.2 (page 98) as conversation starters. As a school leadership team, share your answers, and participate in a discussion on developing your lifelong-learning skills.

Quotes	Discussion Questions
"Anyone who stops learning is old, whether at twenty or eighty. Anyone who keeps learning stays young." —Henry Ford	• What kinds of things do you do to continue to learn? • What kind of learning do you want to engage in during the latter part of your teaching career? • The older you get, do you find it harder or easier to learn new things? Why? • What is (or what do you think will be) your biggest obstacle to learning new things as you get older?
"I have no special talent. I am only passionately curious." —Albert Einstein	• How do you define *passionately curious*? • Do you think learning is a special talent? Why or why not? • When have you been really curious about something in your career? • How are learning and curiosity connected?
"Life is a continuous learning process." —Lailah Gifty Akita	• Why is life "a continuous learning process"? • What benefits are there for continuous learning in life? • How would you define *continuous learning*? • Why do some resist the concept of continuous learning?
"Intellectual growth should commence at birth and cease only at death." —Albert Einstein	• How does intellectual growth tie to lifelong learning? • What is the first professional learning experience you remember as a teacher? How did it help (or not help) you? • Over the course of your career, what has been your best learning experience? What made it effective? • As you get more experienced in your career, what kinds of things do you want to learn about?
"Change is the end result of all true learning." —Leo Buscaglia	• What does change have to do with learning? • Learning must result in change. Why? • Have you ever learned something and not changed as a result? • How would you define *true learning*?
"Continuous learning is the minimum requirement for success in any field." —Brian Tracy	• How are learning and success related? • Why is learning important in education? • How do you engage in continuous learning? • What is your goal for the bare minimum of learning each year?

"Don't let your learning lead to knowledge. Let your learning lead to action." —Jim Rohn	• What is the difference between knowledge and action? • What good is learning if it's just knowledge? • What makes it difficult to turn your learning into action? • What steps can you take to help you turn your learning into action?

FIGURE 7.2: Let's talk about lifelong learning conversation starters.

*Visit **go.SolutionTree.com/PLCbooks** for a free reproducible of this figure.*

Case Scenarios

Use any of the following case scenarios to facilitate a discussion with teacher leaders about the importance of lifelong learning as a teacher leader. After reading the case scenario, encourage participants to discuss how they would respond.

CASE SCENARIO ONE

Teachers in your team are recommending using a unique technology tool for analyzing formative assessment data. One teacher on the team has only used a spreadsheet program for data analysis, and it's all he is comfortable with; he is not open to trying this new tool.

CASE SCENARIO TWO

The team's data analysis shows several students did not master the essential standards. You want to lead a discussion about the teaching strategies members used, and you want to highlight that perhaps the team should look into different strategies since what was done didn't work.

CASE SCENARIO THREE

You attend an amazing conference over the summer and learn a lot of different things, especially about writing quality assessments. However, implementing your new learning will completely change how the team wrote assessments in the past.

CASE SCENARIO FOUR

A teacher in your team is truly knowledgeable about student-engagement strategies. She has studied this topic in depth and even written articles about it. However, her knowledge intimidates others in the team.

Your team participates in book studies and then reads, likes, and forwards articles they see on social media. They also participate in various workshops. However, team members never seem to change any of their practices when they go back to their classroom.

SUBMIT A CASE SCENARIO

Ask teacher leaders to anonymously submit a current scenario that describes their need for professional learning.

The Agree-or-Disagree Line

Invite participants to examine each of the following statements. Allow participants a few minutes to process, and then ask them to stand on the right side of the room if they agree with the statement or the left side of the room if they disagree with the statement. Once participants have chosen their side, open the floor up for discussion by asking, "Why do you agree or disagree with the statement?" The discussion will help participants learn more about the importance of a teacher leader having lifelong-learning skills.

- » **Statement one:** Lifelong learning is easy to say but hard to do.
- » **Statement two:** Time is the biggest barrier for lifelong learning.
- » **Statement three:** The professional development I receive just isn't effective for me to make any changes.
- » **Statement four:** I learn every day when I collaborate with my colleagues. I make changes as a result of these daily experiences.
- » **Statement five:** The longer I teach, the less I feel like I need formal training or workshops.
- » **Statement six:** Lifelong learning means the opposite of status quo.
- » **Statement seven:** Lifelong learning will make me a better educator.

Activity for Developing Lifelong-Learning Skills

A key component to learning is sometimes *unlearning*. You must unlearn what you know to embrace new learning, which is different from what you traditionally have been comfortable with:

> The concept of being a learner has shifted. No more is the concept *learn, do, retire*. To be agile and adaptable, you need to *learn, do, unlearn—learn, do, rest—learn, do, unlearn—repeat*. This is the cycle of a lifelong learner. (Keating, 2020)

Figure 7.3 illustrates the concept of unlearning.

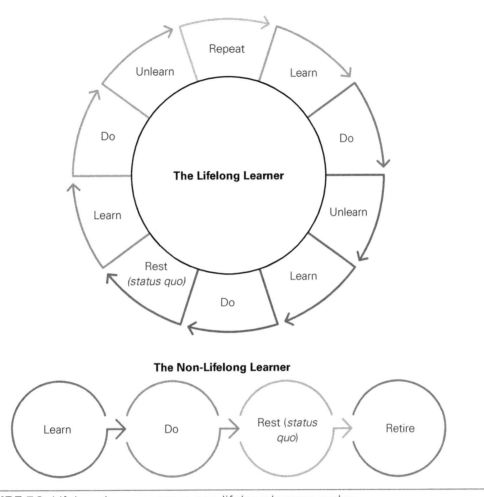

FIGURE 7.3: Lifelong learner versus non-lifelong learner cycles.

The *non-lifelong learner* approach is when you learn something, do it, and remain in status quo until you retire. On the other hand, the *lifelong learner* approach is when you learn something, do it, but realize you must unlearn it, then learn all over again, do it, and stay in status quo for a little while until you realize you must learn again. So to act on that learning, you must unlearn what you previously learned.

Use figure 7.4 (page 102) to identify examples of traditional (or non-lifelong) learning and lifelong learning examples. Think about examples inside and outside education.

Traditional Learner (or Non-Lifelong Learner) Learn, Do, Retire	Lifelong Learner Learn, Do, Unlearn, Learn, Do, Rest, Learn, Do, Unlearn
I learned that **classroom discussion** *was about posing a question to the students. Students who knew the answer would raise their hands so I would call on them, they would answer, and then I'd repeat that process.* *I learned my grading practices were my own decisions based on my own experiences and beliefs about grading.*	*I unlearned what I thought I knew about* **classroom discussion**. *In fact, it is just a conversation between the teacher and the one student who had the answer. I then changed classroom discussions to include strategies that involve all students engaging in answering questions.* *I unlearned what I thought I knew about the "education lottery," which means that a student's grade is dependent on the luck of the draw—or which teacher they are assigned to. My new learning taught me that grading practices must be consistent within my collaborative team, so an A in my class is also an A in another teacher's class. I then changed my grading practices so that, as a team, we had the same grading practices (as it relates to late work, letting students redo work, defining proficiency, and so on) to ensure all students receive consistent feedback and data points, regardless of which teacher they have.*

FIGURE 7.4: Non-lifelong learner versus lifelong learner activity.

Visit **go.SolutionTree.com/PLCbooks** *for a free reproducible of this figure.*

Summary

Lifelong learning is an expectation for all teachers, but especially teacher leaders. Teacher leaders must comfortably and enthusiastically embrace lifelong learning as a way of life to make the impact their schools need. In addition, in a PLC, lifelong learning allows changes in the classroom, as teachers learn from one another and their data. Consider how your school leadership team can use the activities in this chapter to plan your professional learning about developing lifelong-learning skills. It's ironic but true—learning how to be a lifelong learner does require learning!

Reflect on Developing Lifelong-Learning Skills

Pause to reflect on what you've read in this chapter. Use the following prompts to journal about what you learned and next steps you'll take.

Before reading this chapter, how would you have described the relationship between leadership and lifelong learning?

After reading this chapter and participating in the activities, what have you learned about your (or your teacher leaders') lifelong-learning skills?

What do you plan to do to continuously strengthen your (or your teacher leaders') lifelong-learning skills?

Training Teacher Leaders in a PLC at Work® © 2024 Solution Tree Press • SolutionTree.com
Visit **go.SolutionTree.com/PLCbooks** to download this free reproducible.

CHAPTER 8

Developing Emotional Intelligence Skills

Psychologists Peter Salovey and John D. Mayer first introduced and defined the term *emotional intelligence* in 1990:

> A set of skills hypothesized to contribute to the accurate appraisal and expression of emotion in oneself and others, the effective regulation of emotion in self and others, and the use of feelings to motivate, plan, and achieve in one's life. (p. 185)

More simply, *Merriam-Webster* defines *emotional intelligence* (n.d.) as "the ability to recognize, understand, and deal skillfully with one's own emotions and the emotions of others." In other words, *emotional intelligence* refers to your ability to be aware of your emotions as well as being able to manage your own emotions and also the emotions of others.

Psychologist, author, and science journalist Daniel Goleman (1995, 2020) popularized this concept in his best-selling book *Emotional Intelligence: Why It Can Matter More Than IQ*. Goleman (1995, 2020) argues that emotional intelligence is just as important as IQ. You can be incredibly intelligent, but if you are unable to manage your emotions or the emotions of people around you, you may not be as successful. In fact, a CareerBuilder (2011) survey finds 71 percent of employers value emotional intelligence over IQ. "The national survey . . . with more than 2600 hiring managers and human resource professionals—reveals that EI [emotional intelligence] is a critical characteristic for landing a job and advancing one's career." Emotional intelligence is important not only for getting a job and advancing in a job but also for becoming a strong predictor of performance (Landry, 2019). In addition to the many benefits of having high emotional intelligence, coauthors and advocates for teacher well-being Timothy D. Kanold and Tina H. Boogren (2022) discuss *emotional wellness* as a part of overall educator wellness: "we define *educator wellness* as *a continuous, active process toward achieving a positive state of good health and enhanced physical, mental, emotional, and social well-being*" (p. 1). This makes it imperative for teacher leaders to be aware of this important skill to become effective leaders.

In this chapter, I explore five key domains teacher leaders with high emotional intelligence exhibit. Next, I discuss the PLC connection—to all three big ideas (focus on learning, collaborative culture and collective responsibility, and a results orientation). The chapter ends with a series of professional development activities to support teacher leaders to develop emotional intelligence.

Five Key Competencies of Emotional Intelligence

So what makes emotional intelligence so significant that the majority of people deem it as important as (or perhaps even more so than) a person's IQ? Emotional intelligence executive master coach Svetlana Whitener (2022) outlines several advantages people who have high emotional intelligence enjoy.

» They are more likely to name and express their emotions so they are better able to understand and manage their responses to certain events or situations.

» They can identify the root causes of their emotions, which helps them resolve situations instead of just dealing with symptoms.

» They have a good understanding of what drives them and why.

» They remain calm in challenging and stressful situations.

» They can reduce anxiety during stressful times.

» They work well with others.

» They learn from mistakes and criticism.

» They focus on getting better instead of taking things personally.

» They focus on what they have influence or control over.

All other leadership skills I discuss in this book are enhanced when teacher leaders work on developing and strengthening their emotional intelligence as well.

Goleman's (1995, 2020) model of emotional intelligence can help principals support teacher leaders to develop this skill. He states there are five key domains that compose your emotional intelligence, and by strengthening these domains, you can work toward having a higher emotional intelligence (Goleman, 1995, 2020).

1. **Self-awareness:** *Self-awareness* refers to being aware of your emotions as well as the reasons or triggers for those emotions. It's about being aware of how you feel, what caused you to feel that way, and what you do as a result of those emotions. Being aware of your emotions also means you know the impact those emotions will have on others.

2. **Self-regulation:** *Self-regulation* means you are flexible and change your emotions accordingly when you predict the outcome of an emotional reaction. You have the ability to change a negative emotion or feeling into a positive one. You can anticipate what will happen if you express a certain emotion, and as a result, you can alter that emotion. In other words, you do not act on impulse based on the emotion you are experiencing.

3. **Motivation:** *Motivation* refers to your intrinsic desire to meet your personal goals. You want to achieve, so as a result, you are always looking for ways to improve. You genuinely enjoy learning as you see how it gets you closer to your goals. Your internal desire to get better motivates you and, as a result, you are action oriented.

4. **Empathy:** *Empathy* refers to being able to understand how other people feel and what emotions they are experiencing. It helps you bond with your colleagues as you show compassion and understanding. You listen without interrupting because you seek to understand the emotions they are experiencing (even if negative), instead of reacting to their emotions.

5. **Social skills:** *Social skills* refer to your ability to interact with others. You build meaningful relationships because you can elicit trust, communicate well, and connect with others. You are completely comfortable interacting with members of your team, which leads to mutually respectful relationships.

When thinking about how to strengthen each of these five domains to strengthen your overall emotional intelligence, consider the strategies Kanold and Boogren (2022) offer: "Building our emotional wellness includes being aware of how we feel each day; understanding why we feel that way; and reflecting on how we teach, interact with, and lead others, including how we self-regulate our responses to others" (p. 45). To establish action steps to strengthen this leadership skill, it's important to see in what areas you are strong, and in what areas you need to improve.

According to the NHS England, completing the following Leading Across London (2014) questionnaire (see figure 8.1) will give you a sense of where you are in each of the domains of your emotional intelligence. Assess and score each of the statements, with a score of *5* meaning the statement always applies to you and a score of *1* meaning the statement never applies to you.

How much does each statement apply to you?		Score				
1	I realize immediately when I lose my temper.	5	4	3	2	1
2	I can reframe bad situations quickly.	5	4	3	2	1
3	I can always motivate myself to do difficult tasks.	5	4	3	2	1
4	I can always see things from the other person's viewpoint.	5	4	3	2	1
5	I am an excellent listener.	5	4	3	2	1
6	I know when I am happy.	5	4	3	2	1
7	I do not "wear my heart on my sleeve."	5	4	3	2	1
8	I can usually prioritize and get on with important activities at work.	5	4	3	2	1
9	I am excellent at empathizing with someone else's problem.	5	4	3	2	1
10	I never interrupt other people's conversations.	5	4	3	2	1
11	I usually recognize when I am stressed.	5	4	3	2	1
12	Others can rarely tell what kind of mood I am in.	5	4	3	2	1
13	I always meet deadlines.	5	4	3	2	1
14	I can tell if someone is unhappy with me.	5	4	3	2	1
15	I am good at adapting and mixing with a variety of people.	5	4	3	2	1
16	I am aware of when I am being emotional.	5	4	3	2	1
17	I rarely "fly off the handle" at other people.	5	4	3	2	1
18	I never waste time.	5	4	3	2	1
19	I can tell if a team of people are not getting along well.	5	4	3	2	1
20	People are the most interesting thing in life for me.	5	4	3	2	1
21	When I feel anxious, I can usually account for the reason.	5	4	3	2	1
22	Difficult people do not annoy me.	5	4	3	2	1
23	I do not prevaricate.	5	4	3	2	1
24	I can usually understand why people are being difficult toward me.	5	4	3	2	1
25	I love to meet new people and get to know what makes them "tick."	5	4	3	2	1
26	I always know when I'm being unreasonable.	5	4	3	2	1
27	I can consciously alter my frame of mind or mood.	5	4	3	2	1
28	I believe you should do the difficult things first.	5	4	3	2	1
29	Other individuals are not difficult, just different.	5	4	3	2	1

30	I need a variety of work colleagues to make my job interesting.	5	4	3	2	1
31	Awareness of my own emotions at all times is very important to me.	5	4	3	2	1
32	I do not let stressful situations or people affect me once I have left work.	5	4	3	2	1
33	Delayed gratification is a virtue I hold.	5	4	3	2	1
34	I can understand when I am being unreasonable.	5	4	3	2	1
35	I like to ask questions to find out what is important to people.	5	4	3	2	1
36	I can tell if someone has upset or annoyed me.	5	4	3	2	1
37	I rarely worry about work or life in general.	5	4	3	2	1
38	I believe in making what is needed a priority and then making it happen.	5	4	3	2	1
39	I can understand why my actions sometimes offend others.	5	4	3	2	1
40	I see working with difficult people as simply a challenge to win them over.	5	4	3	2	1
41	I can let go of anger quickly so it no longer affects me.	5	4	3	2	1
42	I can suppress my emotions when needed.	5	4	3	2	1
43	I can always motivate myself, even when I feel low.	5	4	3	2	1
44	I can sometimes see things from others' point of view.	5	4	3	2	1
45	I am good at reconciling differences with other people.	5	4	3	2	1
46	I know what makes me happy.	5	4	3	2	1
47	Others often do not know how I am feeling.	5	4	3	2	1
48	Motivation has been the key to my success.	5	4	3	2	1
49	Reasons for disagreements are always clear to me.	5	4	3	2	1
50	I generally build solid relationships with colleagues.	5	4	3	2	1

Record your score from each statement in the following chart.

Self-Awareness		Self-Regulation		Motivation		Empathy		Social Skills	
1		2		3		4		5	
6		7		8		9		10	
11		12		13		14		15	
16		17		18		19		20	
21		22		23		24		25	
26		27		28		29		30	
31		32		33		34		35	
36		37		38		39		40	
41		42		43		44		45	
46		47		48		49		50	

FIGURE 8.1: Domain assessment questionnaire for emotional intelligence.

continued ▶

Next, calculate the total for each of the five domains.

Total =		Total =		Total =		Total =		Total =	
(Self-Awareness)		(Self-Regulation)		(Motivation)		(Empathy)		(Social Skills)	

Use this guide to interpret your totals for each domain.

35–50	This area is a strength for you.
18–34	Give attention to this area.
10–17	Make this a developmental priority.

Finally, record your results.

	Strength	Needs Attention	Priority
Self-Awareness			
Self-Regulation			
Motivation			
Empathy			
Social Skills			

Source: Adapted from Leading Across London, 2014.

Visit **go.SolutionTree.com/PLCbooks** *for a free reproducible of this figure.*

This self-assessment is more comprehensive than the one in the Professional Development Activities section of this chapter (see page 113) because the questionnaire offers teacher leaders the opportunity to identify specific strengths and areas for improvement on each of the emotional intelligence domains.

The PLC Connection: All Three Big Ideas

Emotional intelligence impacts all three big ideas of a PLC, including teacher leaders' ability to lead in a PLC and whether they are focusing on ensuring every practice, policy, and procedure focuses on propelling student learning; confirming high-performing teams are working together on the four critical questions; or creating a culture where data drive change. No matter what aspect of the PLC process teacher leaders are working on, their emotional intelligence is a predictor of success.

State of California mental health programs evaluator and researcher Courtney E. Ackerman (2019) writes, "Leaders have a big job to do in any organization: they need to shape, communicate, and contribute to the organizational vision. Naturally, emotional intelligence helps immensely in this role." Ackerman (2019) goes on to identify several situations and behaviors she labels "vision killers." Each vision killer can deter and stifle the work of a PLC.

As a teacher leader, you lead the PLC work with your colleagues. Think through these vision killers and how having high emotional intelligence will help move your PLC work forward in your team or department.

» "Treating people badly—such as not showing people they care, forgetting to say thank you, not respecting people, not making people feel valued" (Ackerman, 2019).

Think about how this could impact your team as you work together on the second big idea of a PLC—collaborative culture and collective responsibility. When you are trying to help teachers work together, treating them with respect is important for success.

» "Living by the adage 'Do as I say, not as I do,' and not setting good examples" (Ackerman, 2019).

Think about how this could impact your team as you work together on the third big idea of a PLC—a results orientation. You want to set a good example of what it looks like to be vulnerable by openly sharing your data and admitting that perhaps you didn't teach a particular standard as well as you thought. Be open to feedback from your colleagues on how you can get better.

» "Focusing on too many things at once" (Ackerman, 2019).

Think about how this could impact your team as you work together on the first big idea of a PLC—focus on learning. You want to change or tweak all these antiquated practices, policies, and procedures that hinder student learning, but you may end up trying to make too many changes at the same time.

» "Not giving clear direction" (Ackerman, 2019).

Think about how this could impact your team as you work together on the second big idea of a PLC—collaborative culture and collective responsibility. Your team is looking to you for clear directions. For example, your team members need clear direction on how (and why) to prioritize standards, create quality common assessments, and think through the details of providing interventions and enrichment. These are examples of the work your team engages in—but to do them successfully, members need clear direction from you.

» "Focusing on the detail and forgetting to tell the 'whys' or the big picture" (Ackerman, 2019).

Think about how this could impact your team as you work together on the third big idea of a PLC—a results orientation. As your team reviews data, members need to look at the bigger picture or the purpose of looking at data; they must see how they did and what they should do differently next time. The *why* behind looking at data is to see what changes *the teachers* need to make so they can reteach that content.

» "Showing little or no personal commitment to the vision" (Ackerman, 2019).

Think about how this could impact your team as you work together on the first big idea of a PLC—focus on learning. *Focus on learning* means you accept learning as the fundamental purpose of school, which refers to the vision and mission of your school. Teacher leaders must demonstrate their commitment to the school's mission and vision. Everything you do as a teacher leader is to advance that mission and vision (not to maintain adult happiness or the status quo)—ultimately, your commitment is to advance student learning for all.

Teacher leaders need high emotional intelligence to avoid vision killers. As a teacher leader, being aware of your emotions and triggers, being able to regulate your emotions (which means you can dig yourself out of negative emotions), being intrinsically motivated to do the work, understanding the emotions your colleagues experience, and having the ability to develop trusting, mutually respectful relationships are needed to successfully lead the PLC work in your team or department.

PAUSE TO REFLECT

Pause for a moment to reflect on the following questions.

» What kinds of experiences or situations keep teacher leaders from growing their emotional intelligence?

» How does emotional intelligence support teacher leaders to avoid "vision killers" (Ackerman, 2019)?

» How would you describe the importance of emotional intelligence for teacher leaders?

» How will developing your emotional intelligence advance the work of your PLC?

Professional Development Activities for Developing Emotional Intelligence Skills

Now that you've explored the importance of strong emotional intelligence and why it's essential for strong teacher leaders, consider professional development activities to help teacher leaders develop emotional intelligence skills.

Self-Assessment for Emotional Intelligence Skills

A self-assessment is a great way for teacher leaders to reflect on their current reality, specifically their strengths and challenges as it relates to emotional intelligence. Provide teacher leaders the following self-assessment (see figure 8.2) and encourage them to determine specific areas of growth to strengthen this skill.

Instructions: Read each statement and indicate whether it applies to you consistently, usually, occasionally, or rarely. Next, set goals for improving weak aspects of this skill.	Consistently	Usually	Occasionally	Rarely
I become defensive or upset when I receive criticism.	☐	☐	☐	☐
I stay calm under pressure.	☐	☐	☐	☐
I recognize how my emotions and moods impact others.	☐	☐	☐	☐
I always think through things before acting on an impulse because of an emotion.	☐	☐	☐	☐
I have no problem admitting mistakes.	☐	☐	☐	☐
I find it difficult to focus and concentrate when I am upset, angry, or frustrated.	☐	☐	☐	☐
I find it difficult to read other people's emotions.	☐	☐	☐	☐
I establish mutually respectful relationships with everyone.	☐	☐	☐	☐
Look back over your answers. Here, set goals that will support you to improve your emotional intelligence.				

FIGURE 8.2: Assess your emotional intelligence.

*Visit **go.SolutionTree.com/PLCbooks** for a free reproducible of this figure.*

Conversation Starters

Planned conversation starters are a great way to initiate discussions about emotional intelligence and allow participants to learn from peers' diverse perspectives.

Use the quotes and discussion questions in figure 8.3 as conversation starters. As a school leadership team, share your answers, and participate in a discussion on developing your emotional intelligence.

Quotes	Discussion Questions
"There is no separation of mind and emotions; emotions, thinking, and learning are all linked." —Eric Jensen	• How is your mind connected to your emotions? • Can you separate your mind from your emotions? Why or why not? • How do emotions link to thinking? • How do emotions link to learning?
"In a study of skills that distinguish star performers in every field from entry-level jobs to executive positions, the single most important factor was not IQ, advanced degrees, or technical experience, it was EQ [emotional intelligence]. Of the competencies required for excellence in performance in the job studies, 67 percent were emotional competencies." —Daniel Goleman	• Why is emotional intelligence so much more powerful than IQ? • What does this mean for you as a teacher leader? • You have the technical skills to be a teacher leader; in other words, you are a good teacher and probably know and understand the PLC work. What about your emotional intelligence? • What top three emotional competencies do you think are essential for every teacher leader?
"He who smiles rather than rages is always the stronger." —Japanese proverb	• How often do you smile? What kinds of situations make you smile? • How can you make a concerted effort to smile more? • Do you think if you smiled more, it would minimize the negative emotions you experience? Why or why not? • What triggers your anger? How can you control it?
"Any person capable of angering you becomes your master." —Epictetus	• What kinds of things anger you? • What do people do that angers you? • Why does the person who angers you have that kind of power over you? • Do you agree with this quote? Why or why not?
"The sign of an intelligent people is their ability to control their emotions by the application of reason." —Marya Mannes	• How do you control your emotions (good or bad)? • Think of intelligent people you know. How would you describe their emotional intelligence? • How does intelligence relate to your ability to control your emotions? • Why is using the application of reason to help control emotions difficult to do? How do you do it?

"How you react emotionally is a choice in any situation." —Judith Orloff	• Your emotions are a choice. Do you agree or disagree? • How can you think while you react emotionally? • How can reacting emotionally lead to regret? • Having a choice means you are in control. How do you get to that place when emotions are high, intense, or both?
"The emotions of man are stirred more quickly than man's intelligence." —Oscar Wilde	• How are emotions and intelligence connected? • How are emotions "stirred more quickly" than intelligence? • What kinds of things "stir" your emotions? What kinds of things "stir" your intelligence? • In your opinion, which holds more power? Emotions or intelligence? Why?

FIGURE 8.3: Let's talk about emotional intelligence conversation starters.

*Visit **go.SolutionTree.com/PLCbooks** for a free reproducible of this figure.*

Case Scenarios

Use any of the following case scenarios to facilitate a discussion with teacher leaders about the importance of emotional intelligence. After reading the case scenario, ask participants to share how emotional intelligence would support them in the situation.

CASE SCENARIO ONE

You are aware that little things frustrate you very quickly. Those "little things" include people who come in late to work or meetings, people who are so negative, or people who always complain. All these little things annoy you so much! You bottle these emotions up because telling anyone may make you look overly sensitive. You get frustrated when people don't follow through with what they say they will do. You get annoyed during meetings because people seem to talk and talk with no clear purpose. Your feelings of being annoyed, irritated, or frustrated come up frequently.

CASE SCENARIO TWO

It is difficult for you to accept constructive feedback. Being told you did something wrong or working really hard on something only to be told how you can improve or change it is exceedingly difficult to take. You work really hard on everything, so what you're looking for is others' appreciation and recognition. You want to be told you did a really good job because that validates your hard work. But instead, when you are told what you can do to improve or told to make changes, you feel others don't value or recognize your hard work.

CASE SCENARIO THREE

Education is filled with constant stress and pressure. You have parents who watch your every move and purposely email you things because they want your response in writing; they're documenting you. You feel like everyone is waiting for you to make a mistake. The deadlines for paperwork keep coming. The number of calls you must return keeps increasing. The grading to do keeps piling up. This stress is really taking a toll on you.

CASE SCENARIO FOUR

You are greatly confident and assertive. As a result, you say what you need to say because you focus on the work and are committed to always trying to get better. However, not everyone on your team has this same outlook. Some members of your team are sensitive and focus more on having their egos stroked. You don't really care because you know you're "right." The goal is crystal clear for you—increase student achievement. You keep moving forward by pushing through how everyone else feels.

CASE SCENARIO FIVE

You are a people pleaser at heart. You want to make everyone on your team happy and you will do whatever it takes to make that happen. A sense of feeling your team needs you motivates you. Your teammates rely on you, which also motivates you. You need their validation and you love hearing their words of appreciation. A need for others to like you drives you.

SUBMIT A CASE SCENARIO

Ask teacher leaders to anonymously submit a current scenario outlining the importance of emotional intelligence.

The Agree-or-Disagree Line

Invite participants to examine each of the following statements. Allow participants a few minutes to process, and then ask them to stand on the right side of the room if they agree with the statement or the left side of the room if they disagree with the statement. Once they are on their chosen side, open the floor up for discussion by asking, "Why do you agree or disagree with the statement?" The discussion will help participants learn more about the importance of having a teacher leader with high emotional intelligence.

» **Statement one:** When I'm upset, it's difficult to think about anything else.

» **Statement two:** Predicting the outcomes of your actions when you're emotional is hard.

» **Statement three:** Not being able to control your emotions is a sign of weakness (to a certain degree).

» **Statement four:** Emotional intelligence is the glue that holds it altogether. All the other leadership skills students need to succeed are dependent on their emotional intelligence.

» **Statement five:** Accepting criticism, admitting mistakes, and apologizing in public are understandably humiliating and embarrassing; they can easily be a blow to your self-esteem.

» **Statement six:** There are days I get irritated quicker. Something a student does or something a colleague says just irritates me; it's hard to explain why.

» **Statement seven:** The older I get, the less I care about what others think. That means the older I get, the higher my emotional intelligence.

Activity to Strengthen Emotional Intelligence Skills

Temperament can play a part in a person's emotional intelligence. A person's *temperament* is biological rather than learned; it is "an aspect of personality concerned with emotional dispositions and reactions and their speed and intensity" (Emotional intelligence, n.d.). Examples include being a social butterfly who loves talking to people or an introvert who needs alone time to recharge. Teacher leaders benefit from being aware of their temperament because it determines their emotional reactions to whatever is happening around them (Yilmaz, 2023). A physician (Galen of Pergamon) in the second century AD developed the classic four temperaments (as cited in Yilmaz, 2023).

1. **Sanguine:** Talkative, friendly, carefree, sociable, outgoing, and lively
2. **Choleric:** Assertive, ambitious, and goal-oriented
3. **Melancholic:** Reserved, quiet, thoughtful, analytical, cautious, and introspective
4. **Phlegmatic:** Calm, easy-going, even-tempered, content, and peaceful

Encourage teacher leaders to complete the activity in figure 8.4 (page 118) to learn about their temperament and understand how it impacts their emotional intelligence.

1. Describe your temperament with three adjectives that describe you best.
2. Suggest three adjectives that others use to describe your temperament.
3. How does each of the temperamental factors affect you on a personal level?
4. How does each of the temperamental factors affect you on a leadership role level?
5. Which of these factors do you want to change and why?

Source: Adapted from Skills Converged, 2017.

FIGURE 8.4: Emotional intelligence strengthening activity.

*Visit **go.SolutionTree.com/PLCbooks** for a free reproducible of this figure.*

Instruct participants to choose a partner, and give the pairs ten minutes to share their responses with each other.

As a large teacher leader team, engage in a discussion using the following questions.

» What do you think of the effect of your temperament on your everyday life?

» How did your partner's temperament differ from yours?

» Was it easy to come up with strategies on how to change or modify some of the discussed behaviors?

» How does your specific temperament relate to your emotional intelligence?

Because temperament is biological and emotional intelligence is learned, acknowledging your temperament can help build your emotional intelligence. Understanding and discussing your temperament can also be a helpful way to start thinking about how to strengthen your emotional intelligence.

Summary

Emotional intelligence is essential for leadership. Teacher leaders should always be striving to strengthen their emotional intelligence because it will make every other leadership skill much more effective and productive. "Emotional intelligence begins with the ability to accept your emotions and manage them in order to eliminate stress and handle life's difficulties" (Draghici, 2023). By minimizing stress and having the ability to handle challenges, teacher leaders can overcome any barrier as they lead their team or department with high emotional intelligence. Consider how your school leadership team can use the activities in this chapter to plan your professional learning about developing emotional intelligence.

REPRODUCIBLE

Reflect on Developing Emotional Intelligence Skills

Pause to reflect on what you've read in this chapter. Use the following prompts to journal about what you learned and next steps you'll take.

Before reading this chapter, how would you have described the relationship between leadership and emotional intelligence?

After reading this chapter and participating in the activities, what have you learned about your (or your teacher leaders') emotional intelligence skills?

What do you plan to do to continuously strengthen your (or your teacher leaders') emotional intelligence skills?

CHAPTER 9

Developing Change-Leadership Skills

Think about the PLC workshops or professional development conferences you (or your staff) have attended. What happens after you (or they) return? Do you notice sustainable change, or do things eventually go back to the way they've always been?

Now imagine that you (or your staff) attend professional learning opportunities with the expectation to commit to making at least two sustainable changes. What two things will change because of their learning?

Learning equals change. If what you learn doesn't translate into changing your behavior, then learning did not occur. The excitement you felt during that conference and the great ideas you brought back aren't worth much if they don't translate into new or different ways of working. In other words, change is necessary for improvement. Not changing anything means you choose to perpetuate the status quo and forfeit improvement.

The commitment to continuous improvement in a PLC means teacher leaders must be able to influence their peers. A culture that calls teams to continually look for ways to change the status quo relies on inspiring, persistent, and trustworthy leaders. Teacher leaders in a PLC drive innovation and change. Therefore, possessing change-leadership skills is a must for teacher leaders in a PLC.

In this chapter, I explore eight steps teacher leaders can follow to successfully lead change. Next, I discuss the PLC connection—specifically to big idea number one (focus on learning). The chapter ends with a series of professional development activities to support teacher leaders to develop the skill of leading change.

Eight Steps for Leading Change

Change can be difficult for many different reasons. Change requires a lot of work, takes time and effort, can be exhausting, and brings up emotions like fear and uncertainty. Leadership expert Douglas Reeves (2021), author of *Deep Change Leadership: A Model for Renewing and Strengthening Schools and Districts*, explains one of the reasons change is so difficult: "The root of resistance to change is that even when we want change, we are confronting the fact that we are not acceptable as we are" (p. 30). Humans in general, and educators in particular, don't want to accept the idea they're unacceptable or not enough. And they don't like discomfort—people prefer doing things they already know and are comfortable with. Trying something new inevitably makes people nervous or afraid they'll fail because they've never done it before and don't know how it will turn out.

However, if educators refuse to change, they will never get better—which doesn't support the work of a PLC, which includes dedication to continuous improvement. Teacher leaders in a PLC must practice moving through the discomfort of change as well as navigating their colleagues' resistance to change.

Effectively leading change is a critical skill teacher leaders need to effectively guide their colleagues. Kotter (n.d.) outlines an eight-step process principals may find helpful in supporting teacher leaders to navigate change. Even if the change is coming from the top, teacher leaders are closer to the action, so they need to know how to lead their departments or teams through change.

1. **Create a sense of urgency:** Know the *why* behind the change. Before teacher leaders implement a change, they must understand the rationale. And that *why* cannot be "because our administration wants us to do this." Teacher leaders need to own the reason for the change and be able to explain it in a way that their colleagues understand how it will benefit students.

2. **Build a guiding coalition:** Just as school administrators secure buy-in with teacher leaders when implementing change, teacher leaders must secure buy-in with the teachers on their teams. This is sometimes a work in

progress, so even if initially teacher leaders can only get buy-in from one or two colleagues, it's an essential early step.

3. **Form a strategic vision:** While administrators form a strategic vision for the whole school, teacher leaders provide a strategic vision to illustrate how their department or team will implement the change to further the school's strategic vision to positively impact students. Teacher leaders forming strategic visions for their departments or teams ensure alignment with the school's vision.

4. **Enlist a volunteer "army":** Change is a collective effort. Teacher leaders need as many teachers as possible from their department or team to rally around the common goal for the change. Teacher leaders should identify who their biggest supporters will be for that change and enlist them to be the change's cheerleaders. These teachers will not only support the change but also help teacher leaders implement the change.

5. **Enable action by removing barriers:** Each department or team will encounter different obstacles to implementation. Teacher leaders must identify potential barriers and seek solutions to ensure the change is successful. For example, one barrier could be to identify potential resisters to the change. Once identified, teacher leaders brainstorm ways to work with the resisters one-to-one prior to implementing the change with the goal of winning them over.

6. **Generate short-term wins:** Educators often neglect to celebrate the small wins, which is important for sustainability and teacher well-being. When planning the change, teacher leaders should think about when and how their team will celebrate small wins. Don't wait for the change to be complete before celebrating. The small wins along the journey keep the momentum and motivation going throughout the change process.

7. **Sustain acceleration:** In addition to celebrating small wins, teacher leaders must keep the vision top of mind so the implementation doesn't stall. Successful implementation relies on consistent momentum. Teacher leaders should build in time for team members to reflect on the change. What is going well with the process? What needs improvement or adjustment? Identify when and how colleagues will engage with this process of reflection.

8. **Institute the change:** This is the hard part. How do teacher leaders ensure the change stays in place instead of reverting back to the more

comfortable way of doing things? Teacher leaders should design routines and systems that consistently show how the change is leading to student success. This brings the team full-circle, tying their efforts back to the *why* to ensure sustainable change. The goal is that even if there is a change in school administration, with teacher leaders leading changes in their departments, those changes should stay for the long haul, regardless of who is in administration.

Remember, change is *hard*. If school administrators expect teacher leaders to lead change in their teams or departments, they need the support and training to lead well. Sending teacher leaders to a professional learning workshop and hoping they'll come back equipped to implement sustainable change is not an effective strategy. Follow the eight-step change process I outline in this chapter and use the professional development activities to develop change-leadership skills among your teacher leaders.

The PLC Connection: Focus on Learning

The purpose of a PLC is to improve student learning—to get more students to learn at high levels, become college or career ready, and grow into productive citizens. But none of this will happen without change. Consider professor emeritus at Middle Tennessee State University Robert Eaker's (2020) view on leading change in a PLC:

> One aspect of becoming a PLC is clear: school leaders must *successfully lead the change process*. Perhaps the greatest barrier to becoming a PLC is that while there may be widespread agreement, and even enthusiasm, regarding PLCs as a *concept*, there will often be deeper opposition to real change. (p. 140)

Change is inevitable with anything you do when working in a PLC. The first big idea of a PLC is *focus on learning*, which means every practice, policy, and procedure is based on what is best for student learning. When a collaborative team recognizes a practice, policy, or procedure that has nothing to do with student learning, it's time to change it.

Many existing practices, policies, and procedures are designed with *adults* in mind. School and district leaders maintain practices, policies, and procedures because they keep adults happy and comfortable, or maintain the status quo. The mindset of "this is the way we've always done it" is powerful. As a teacher leader, think about the practices you currently use in your department or team. Are those practices actively improving student learning? Or did those practices improve student learning ten years ago? When was the last time you gathered and analyzed data on those practices?

For example, say your middle school has a program for student recognition. The program has been in place for many years and educators have not revised or analyzed the program in fifteen years. Is the program impacting student learning? You reflect on whether those recognition practices motivate students the way recognitions should. You realize the practices only recognize *academic* achievement, so the same students get recognized every quarter (for getting straight As or the best test grades). This is great, but what if, as a teacher leader, you changed your department's recognition practices to also include recognition of students who showed *growth*—for example, the student who gained 135 points on a district benchmark assessment. Although she may be a "below basic" student, her score went up from 65 points to 200 points. That's a huge jump you should celebrate! Or the student who ran the most laps or completed the most push-ups in physical education—maybe that student gets an Athlete of the Month award. Some of these students may never get recognized for high academic achievement, but the progress they're making in other areas is worth celebrating. The antiquated practice of only recognizing the top achievers leaves out many students who demonstrate successes in other ways, so it's probably time to change that practice.

Here's something else to consider: Is it worthwhile to make changes just for the sake of changing things up? Think about initiatives. Leaders bring on new initiatives all the time, but how often do they review the results of those initiatives? Or how often do they comprehensively research the initiative before implementing it in their school? Do leaders create an appropriate monitoring plan to examine an initiative's impact on student learning? In most cases, initiatives pile on top of other initiatives because leaders are eager to make too many changes. Former school principal Peter DeWitt (2021) writes about the implications for staff: "What this means is that the longer teachers and leaders have been working in their school, the more they have seen initiatives come and go and begin to lose faith in the process, so the initiative, whether it's good or bad, loses steam before it even begins." Staff disillusionment impacts students as the educators' focus is no longer on what is best for student learning. Staff can easily fall into the trap of avoiding change to perpetuate the status quo, or making too many changes without a monitoring plan to review the impact of the change on student learning.

When educators think about focus on learning in a PLC (big idea number one), collaborative teams should examine their current practices, policies, and procedures, and then assess if and how they are improving student learning. If they are not impacting student learning, then consider changing your practices. However, don't make changes just for the sake of changing something. Leadership teams should examine how practices, policies, and procedures impact student learning before, during, and after implementing any change. The practice of keeping things the way they are because "this is how we've always done it" must change; leaders should undertake new initiatives and commit to monitoring their effects on student learning.

PAUSE TO REFLECT

Pause for a moment to reflect on the following questions.

» What are your thoughts on Kotter's (n.d.) eight-step process for leading change? How might his model support teacher leaders to lead change?

» Have you attended a conference or workshop and come back energized— but then changed nothing about your practice (or have you seen this tendency in teacher leaders)? Why or why not?

» Why do teacher leaders need to develop the skill of leading change?

» How will developing change-leadership skills advance the work of your PLC?

Professional Development Activities for Leading Change

Now that you've explored the importance of leading change and why it's an essential skill for strong teacher leaders, consider professional development activities to help teacher leaders develop the skill of leading change.

Self-Assessment for Change-Leadership Skills

A self-assessment is a great way for teacher leaders to reflect on their current reality when it comes to leading change, specifically their strengths and challenges. Provide teacher leaders the self-assessment in figure 9.1 about their change leadership and encourage them to determine specific areas for growth to strengthen this skill.

Instructions: Read each statement and indicate whether it applies to you consistently, usually, occasionally, or rarely. Next, set goals for improving weak aspects of this skill.				
	Consistently	**Usually**	**Occasionally**	**Rarely**
I hesitate to make changes until I know everything will go exactly as planned.	☐	☐	☐	☐

I look forward to changes; changes are exciting.	☐	☐	☐	☐
I'm willing to risk disapproval from my colleagues to make changes needed to better my department or team.	☐	☐	☐	☐
The hardest part about change is convincing everyone in my department or team that the change is for the better.	☐	☐	☐	☐
Whenever I see something that needs to be better, I begin planning for that change right away.	☐	☐	☐	☐
I want my colleagues to be comfortable with the change before I implement the change.	☐	☐	☐	☐
I prepare for change by predicting which teachers will have the hardest time with it and proactively work with those teachers.	☐	☐	☐	☐
Look back over your answers. Here, set goals that will support you to improve your ability to lead change.				

FIGURE 9.1: Assess your change-leadership skills.

Visit go.SolutionTree.com/PLCbooks for a free reproducible of this figure.

Conversation Starters

Planned conversation starters are a great way to initiate discussions about change leadership and allow participants to learn from peers' diverse perspectives on leading change.

Use the quotes and discussion questions in figure 9.2 (page 128) as conversation starters. As a school leadership team, share your answers, and participate in a discussion on developing your change-leadership skills.

Quotes	Discussion Questions
"If you want to make enemies, try to change something." —Woodrow Wilson	• What is the worst thing you think your colleagues will do if you try to change something in your department or grade level? • What do you think Wilson means by "enemies"? • Describe a time when others made you an "enemy" because you tried to change something. • Why would someone in your department or grade level make you an "enemy" if you tried to change something?
"The key to change is to let go of fear." —Rosanne Cash	• Why are people in your department or grade level afraid of change? • What can you do to help your department or grade-level team "let go of fear"? • What kinds of changes are people most fearful of? • What kinds of changes are people least fearful of?
"Your success in life isn't based on your ability to simply change. It is based on your ability to change faster than your competition, customers, and business." —Mark Sanborn	• How does this quote relate to schools? • What skills do you need to "change faster"? • What slows down the change process in your department or grade level? • Who is your competition? Who are your customers? What is your business? How do you change faster than them?
"The measure of intelligence is the ability to change." —Albert Einstein	• How does the ability to change relate to intelligence? • How can you use intelligence to successfully lead change? • What can you do to strengthen your intelligence before leading a change? • Describe people who hate change. How do you lead them?
"If you don't like something, change it. If you can't change it, change your attitude." —Maya Angelou	• Make a list of the things people in your department or grade level want you (as their leader) to change. Which of those changes will not happen because they are beyond your control? • When should you try to change your attitude? When should you try to change the attitudes of the people in your department or grade-level team? • What steps would you take to facilitate changing something you don't like in your department or grade level? • How would you lead the process for a change that you personally don't agree with but are responsible for?

"I cannot say whether things will get better if we change; what I can say is they must change if they are to get better." —Georg C. Lichtenberg	• What is the problem with not changing? • What makes you open to change versus resistant to change? • Why do organizations need change? • What would happen in your school, department, or grade level if nothing ever changed?
"All great changes are preceded by chaos." —Deepak Chopra	• How would you describe the "chaos" that precedes change on your campus? • Reflect on the changes made in your school in the last five years. What changes went well and what changes did not go well? • As a leader, what steps can you take to minimize the chaos that occurs before a change? • What is the most important first step to help minimize chaos?

FIGURE 9.2: Let's talk about change leadership conversation starters.

*Visit **go.SolutionTree.com/PLCbooks** for a free reproducible of this figure.*

Case Scenarios

Case scenarios are a great tool leaders can use to imagine how they would lead change in different situations. Use any of the following case scenarios to facilitate a discussion about change leadership. After reading the case scenario, have the school leadership team members each share how they would lead that particular change.

CASE SCENARIO ONE

To help improve student behavior in classrooms, you want to create department or grade-level classroom-management expectations. You want consistency, so the same expectations exist in every classroom. In addition, you want to ensure teachers handle all violations the same way. You will be asking the teachers on your team to change how they have historically handled disruptions in their classroom, and collaborate to establish consistent teacher expectations and responses when students violate those expectations.

CASE SCENARIO TWO

You realize if your team is going to use data points to determine which students need extra help and which students need enrichment, you must ensure your data points accurately reflect what the students learned relating to the standards. You want to change grading practices in your department (or team) so teachers only give grades for the specific standards they are teaching or assessing. In other words, no more giving bonus points for turning work in early or bringing supplies to the classroom, and no more taking points away for turning work in late or any other kind of "bad" behavior.

CASE SCENARIO THREE

Teachers on your campus refuse to identify essential standards because they believe all standards are essential. You must change their thinking because you realize the interventions your team provides are not effective since teachers in your department (or team) are trying to reteach everything. You want to make those interventions effective by ensuring teachers effectively answer question one of the PLC process (What do we want all students to learn?). This means teachers moving from the usual practice of treating all standards as essential to unpacking and understanding the standards and then identifying which are absolutely essential.

CASE SCENARIO FOUR

You've done some research on renowned author John Hattie's (2023) work with visible learning, and learned about how these instructional strategies have a significant impact on student learning. One strategy is *student self-reported grading*, which includes students setting goals and tracking their progress toward meeting those goals. You know your teachers will see this as a lot of work; the logistics of how to do it for each of their students for every unit can be daunting. There are other teachers in your department (or team) who feel they already do this, but you know it's not being done with the specificity or frequency it should be. For example, you want students to specifically set goals and track their progress on essential standards in each of the units, but some teachers have students set goals for their final grade in the class or their end-of-year state assessment.

CASE SCENARIO FIVE

Teachers in your department (or team) have been complaining a lot about student behavior lately; student behavior is just not what it needs to be. Every time you ask teachers if they called the parents, their answer is, "There's no point" or "I sent an email and the parent just got upset." Teachers want to write the office referrals and hope administrators will do something. You want the teachers to take ownership for communicating with parents first. You also want teachers to recognize the students exhibiting positive behavior. But the students exhibiting negative behaviors are overwhelming teachers.

Ask teacher leaders to anonymously submit a current scenario that describes a change they want to implement or a change they saw another person implement well or not so well.

The Agree-or-Disagree Line

Invite participants to examine each of the following statements. Allow participants a few minutes to process, and then ask them to stand on the right side of the room if they agree with the statement or the left side of the room if they disagree with the statement. Once participants have chosen their side, open the floor up for discussion by asking, "Why do you agree or disagree with the statement?" The discussion will help participants learn more about the importance of a teacher leader having change-leadership skills.

» **Statement one:** Being the best leader I can be means absolutely hating the status quo.

» **Statement two:** Change is a constant in leadership, so I must embrace change to be an effective leader.

» **Statement three:** I don't know if leading change is really my job as a teacher leader.

» **Statement four:** I want administrators to tell me what change I need to implement, and then I'll implement it with my department or team.

» **Statement five:** I have no authority to tell my department or team to change anything.

» **Statement six:** I don't know where to begin when thinking about changing things in my department (or team).

» **Statement seven:** I have a hard time trying to balance changing things with preserving the past and how "we've always done it" because our results have been fine.

Leading-Change Journal Activity

No doubt each department (or team) in your school is composed of many diverse personalities. This activity will help teacher leaders identify how their colleagues process change. Begin by giving your teacher leaders each a copy of figure 9.3 (page 132), emphasizing this is a private activity—for their eyes only. Explain that *ambassadors* are the teachers in their departments (or teams) who will be in favor of the change, and *resisters* are teachers who will resist the change. *Neutrals* are the teachers who could go either way—they might support or resist the change. Treat this activity as a journal prompt to support teacher leaders to brainstorm action steps for their colleagues. Have participants each write the names of their colleagues in each column. After completing the activity, participants respond to the reflection questions.

Instructions: Think about an upcoming change in your department (or team). Write the names of colleagues you believe will process the change as *ambassadors* (will support the change), *resisters* (will resist the change), or *neutrals* (will be neutral about the change).		
Ambassador	**Resister**	**Neutral**
How can you enlist the ambassadors to support your change efforts?		
How can you address the concerns of resisters to minimize conflict?		
How might you clarify the need for change to get buy-in from neutrals?		

FIGURE 9.3: Leading-change activity.

*Visit **go.SolutionTree.com/PLCbooks** for a free reproducible of this figure.*

As a school leadership team, brainstorm specific activities for each group of teacher leaders to help prepare them for the change. The goal is to have members of the school leadership team collaborate with one another so they become better change agents for their departments and teams. The members learn and share ideas about how they will lead their colleagues—some who will be cheerleaders for the change and others, maybe not so much.

Summary

Leading change is a critical skill teacher leaders must develop. Too many times, teacher leaders are charged with leading change without knowing how to do it successfully and sustainably. Change is an inevitable part of school leadership. PLCs are committed to continuous improvement, believing teams can always get better. But teachers cannot get better if they continue to do things the same way, no matter how comfortable they are with the status quo. Remember learning equals change. If teacher leaders expect to learn and grow as professionals, then change is a natural by-product of that learning experience. Consider how your school leadership team can use the activities in this chapter to plan your professional learning about developing change leadership.

REPRODUCIBLE

Reflect on Developing Change-Leadership Skills

Pause to reflect on what you've read in this chapter. Use the following prompts to journal about what you learned and next steps you'll take.

Before reading this chapter, how would you have described the relationship between leadership and change-leadership skills?

After reading this chapter and participating in the activities, what have you learned about your (or your teacher leaders') change-leadership skills?

What do you plan to do to continuously strengthen your (or your teacher leaders') change-leadership skills?

CHAPTER 10

Developing Innovation Skills

Innovation is a way of thinking that allows leaders to generate new ideas or different ways to make something better. Educator and speaker George Couros (2015) defines *innovative leadership* as the ability to both create and influence others to create new and better ideas to move toward positive results. *Being innovative* means moving away from the status quo *to get better*, not just for the sake of doing something new or different:

> Different for the sake of different can be a waste of time and may even leave us worse off than where we started. Simply replacing "A" with "B" is not only not innovation but it could actually lead to something worse than what we had before. (Couros, 2015, p. 26)

Education is evolving ever more rapidly. While many changes are positive and support educators' work, many changes—such as the global pandemic and the rise of AI—pose unprecedented challenges and unforeseen opportunities that require innovative solutions. Educators must apply creativity and imagination to design solutions that ensure students continue to thrive. Educator and scholar Sara J. Baker (2022) writes, "As leaders, it is your responsibility to create an environment where people feel comfortable exploring new ideas or taking risks; without this type of leadership, organizations will never progress past being stuck with old ideas and old methods."

Innovation requires educational leaders to think of the educational system differently. In fact, the concept of training teacher leaders to lead itself is innovative. As I posit in chapter 2 (page 21), teacher leaders are traditionally seen as *representatives* of their department or team; the idea that they are *leaders* responsible for change is new (Livingston, 1992). The transformation of the role of teacher leader is an example of innovation. How might teacher leaders draw on innovation to move their departments and teams toward school improvement instead of perpetuating the status quo?

In this chapter, I explore practices to help teacher leaders grow their ability to innovate. Next I discuss the PLC connection—specifically to big idea number one (focus on learning). The chapter ends with a series of professional development activities to support teacher leaders to develop innovation.

Practices for Developing Innovation

Building teacher leaders' capacity to be innovative means cultivating a mindset so educators don't settle for "good enough." An innovative leader continuously looks for ways to improve rather than being comfortable with the way things are. Teacher leaders should actively look for ways to improve rather than being satisfied with the status quo. Following are practices teacher leaders can adopt to encourage innovation.

» **Embrace failure:** Fear of failure is a common barrier to innovation. Maintaining the status quo feels *comfortable*. Trying a new idea might make things better, but what if it doesn't? What if it makes things worse? To overcome fear of failure, teacher leaders should practice accepting failure not as a problem but as a pathway to growth and insight. Writing for the *HYPE Innovation Blog*, account manager Maria Wenning (2017) notes: "It is only through failing that you learn to get outside the box and find the ingredients for innovation that everyone else is missing." Think of your own past failures and the innovations that came from them. Imagine the possible breakthroughs if every teacher leader on your campus gained the capacity to embrace failure as fuel for innovation.

» **Ask questions:** Encourage teacher leaders to get into the habit of asking questions. Asking questions forces leaders to think differently, sparking new thoughts and ideas. For example, teacher leaders can practice asking questions such as, "What if we did it another way?" "Why do we do it this way?" or "What factors could we change that we haven't tried before?" As educators, it's tempting to be content with the way things are. But teacher leaders each must practice training their mind to ask questions as a path to innovation. Think about how much educators encourage students to ask questions; that's because they know asking questions encourages students to explore familiar concepts in new ways.

» **Brainstorm:** Brainstorming is a great way for teacher leaders to begin to strengthen their innovation skills. Dave Wendland (2023), vice president of strategic relations at Hamacher Resource Group (HRG), points to *nonjudgment* as a key factor in successfully generating new ideas: "Brainstorming is commonly a free flow of ideas during which participants produce as many solutions or concepts as possible without criticism or judgment." Seeing all the reasons why something *won't* work can sometimes get in the way of identifying innovative solutions. Work with teacher leaders to delay skepticism during the brainstorming phase to maximize generation of new ideas. Set aside time for brainstorming sessions with teacher leaders and model the process. Designating time for brainstorming and modeling the process supports participants to focus on the task at hand, generate a free flow of ideas, put aside distractions, and cultivate an innovative mindset. Wendland (2023) states that brainstorming is the most valuable way for any organization to encourage innovation.

» **Give credit:** Environment plays an important role in nurturing innovation—if teacher leaders aren't confident they will get credit for their ideas, they will be reluctant to share. To create an environment of trust, give credit every time credit is due. Baker (2022) writes that "the best leaders are ones that look for opportunities to give teammates the credit they deserve when an innovative solution is discovered or implemented." Therefore, when teacher leaders hesitate to share ideas, principals should take their hesitation as a cue to consider how to boost trust and appropriate recognition among staff. Doing so will motivate teacher leaders to innovate and share ideas without fear of someone else getting the credit. When leading your team, especially during brainstorming sessions, be aware of *who* is generating ideas—especially the ideas the team ends up using—and find ways to give those members credit for innovation.

Innovation isn't about reinventing the wheel every time, but rather, thinking about new or alternative ways of doing things. Futurist and innovation speaker Robert Tucker (2017) writes: "Innovation in the next economy is about much more than inventing. It's about figuring out how and where you can add unique value. It's about how fast you can unlearn, relearn and master new skills." The willingness to unlearn and relearn is what innovation is all about. Teacher leaders must foster a mindset that challenges the status quo, embraces diverse ideas, and seeks to change practices, policies, and procedures to ensure achievement for all students.

The PLC Connection: Focus on Learning

Ensuring all students learn at high levels involves challenging the status quo. Principals and teacher leaders in a PLC must always examine and question current practices, policies, and procedures in light of their impact on student learning and identify opportunities for innovation when they are no longer working.

For example, a school has had an intervention block in their schedule for five years. Staff use that time during the school day to help students who fail to master the essential standards. The school staff made significant gains their first few years after implementing this practice. However, since then, the intervention block has turned into a study hall, where students work on late assignments or make up missing work. The practice is not working the way educators intended. Committed to their work as a PLC, the principal and teacher leaders work together to critically examine the practice to optimize student learning; they seek innovative ways to make the intervention block more impactful for students.

Innovation requires critical thinking, which is essential to the first big idea of a PLC (focus on learning). Teacher leaders critically examine the current practices, policies, and procedures to determine their impact on student learning. Are your school's practices, policies, and procedures advancing student achievement? If not, then how can your leadership team draw on its creativity to explore innovative solutions? It's also important to consider the solutions you create are not permanent; initiatives that work best now will likely only be relevant for a few years. That's what a commitment to continuous improvement is all about. Innovation never stops in a PLC because all staff continuously strive to advance learning for all students in a rapidly evolving world. This commitment requires teacher leaders in a PLC to develop innovation skills.

PAUSE TO REFLECT

Pause for a moment to reflect on the following questions.

» Which strategies will be most successful in encouraging teacher leaders to embrace innovation?

» How might innovative teacher leaders improve their team or department?

» What challenges do teacher leaders face to becoming innovative?

» How will developing innovation skills advance the work of your PLC?

Professional Development Activities for Developing Innovation Skills

Now that you've explored the importance of innovation and why it's essential for strong teacher leaders, consider professional development activities to help teacher leaders develop innovation skills.

Self-Assessment for Innovation Skills

A self-assessment is a great way for teacher leaders to reflect on their current reality, specifically their strengths and challenges. Provide teacher leaders the self-assessment in figure 10.1 and encourage them to determine specific areas of growth to strengthen their innovation skills.

Instructions: Read each statement and indicate whether it applies to you consistently, usually, occasionally, or rarely. Next, set goals for improving weak aspects of this skill.	Consistently	Usually	Occasionally	Rarely
I come up with creative ideas to solve problems.	☐	☐	☐	☐
I like to think outside the box.	☐	☐	☐	☐
I enjoy experimenting with new ideas.	☐	☐	☐	☐
I see problems from different perspectives and come up with a variety of solutions.	☐	☐	☐	☐
I identify emerging trends and ideas.	☐	☐	☐	☐
I am always looking for ways to innovate and improve our current practices.	☐	☐	☐	☐
I am deeply committed to continuous improvement.	☐	☐	☐	☐
I value learning new things so I can be creative with leading the PLC work.	☐	☐	☐	☐
Look back over your answers. Here, set goals that will support you to improve your ability to innovate.				

FIGURE 10.1: Assess your innovation skills.

*Visit **go.SolutionTree.com/PLCbooks** for a free reproducible of this figure.*

Conversation Starters

Planned conversation starters are a great way to initiate discussions about innovation and allow participants to learn from peers' diverse perspectives.

Use the quotes and discussion questions in figure 10.2 as conversation starters. As a school leadership team, share your answers, and participate in a discussion on developing your innovation skills.

Quotes	Discussion Questions
"Innovation distinguishes between a leader and a follower." —Steve Jobs	• Why does a leader need to be innovative? • Why does a follower not need to be innovative? • What are other differences between *leaders* and *followers*? • How is innovation different in education compared to businesses (such as Apple)?
"There's a way to do it better—find it." —Thomas Edison	• What are some things your team or department could improve? • How can you identify things that need improvement? • How do you find a way "to do it better" when something has always been done the same way? • Is there always a way "to do it better"? Why or why not?
"Creativity is thinking up new things. Innovation is doing new things." —Theodore Levitt	• How are creativity and innovation linked? • Are you more creative or innovative? Why? • Is it easier for people to be thinkers or doers when it comes to creativity and innovation? Why? • What prevents you from doing new things?
"If you always do what you always did, you will always get what you always got." —Albert Einstein	• Why do educators continue to do "what [they] always did"? • What is something you and your team or department could improve that you "always did"? • Why is getting "what you always got" a bad thing? • How can this quote inspire you to be innovative?
"If you want something new, you have to stop doing something old." —Peter Drucker	• Do you want something new for your team or department? Why or why not? • Is it easy for you to stop doing something old? Why or why not? • What is an effective strategy to stop doing something that has always been done to make room for innovation? • Why is it a bad idea to do something new without stopping something old?

"Innovation is taking two things that already exist and putting them together in a new way." —Tom Freston	• How would you define *innovation*? • What two things can you think of in your team or department you could put together in a new way? • Is it easier to work with existing ideas or come up with new ideas? Why? • How can you look at current practices in your team or department in a different way?
"Innovation is the only way to win." —Steve Jobs	• Are innovation and winning connected? Why or why not? • How do you handle the pressure of being innovative? • What is the most innovative idea you have seen in education? What made it so innovative? What were the results on student achievement? • Without innovation, how else can a school "win"?

FIGURE 10.2: Let's talk about innovation conversation starters.

*Visit **go.SolutionTree.com/PLCbooks** for a free reproducible of this figure.*

Case Scenarios

Use any of the following case scenarios to facilitate a discussion with teacher leaders about the importance of innovative thinking or addressing barriers to innovation. After reading the case scenario, discuss how innovation supports teacher leaders in navigating this situation.

CASE SCENARIO ONE

You want to engage your team (or department) in brainstorming ideas to make it better. You decide to schedule some time for brainstorming in your monthly meetings. You're excited to do this because you see the importance of innovation in school improvement. As your team (or department) members begin these brainstorming sessions, you find your colleagues do not participate in the way you thought they would. They don't generate ideas the way you expected.

CASE SCENARIO TWO

You are struggling with being innovative. You don't know how to come up with ideas to make things better in your team (or department). You are aware of ways the status quo is not serving students, but you struggle to come up with new ways. For example, what new strategy can you use to help students come to class on time or turn in their work on time? Or what new template can your team use to analyze common assessment data?

Or what new reteaching strategy can your team use to help students? You want to be an innovative leader, but you struggle to know *how*. You are used to following the rules and perpetuating the status quo. The idea of coming up with innovative ideas as a teacher leader is new to you. You're not sure how to start.

CASE SCENARIO THREE

There are so many different strengths and skills represented in your team (or department); each team member has something unique to offer. For instance, one member is logical and skilled at thinking through all the details. Another team member is visionary and skilled at thinking in terms of big-picture ideas. Another easily identifies barriers to implementation, and alerts the rest of the team (or department) to potential pitfalls. To be innovative, you know you must pull from the many diverse strengths and skills in your team (or department), but you're not sure how.

CASE SCENARIO FOUR

To embrace innovation, you realize you must ask the right questions at the right time. You understand the importance of asking, "What if we do this?" or "What would happen if we tried it this way?" At the same time, though, you don't want to overwhelm your team (or department) members. You wonder how to find the right balance of asking the right questions at the right time to encourage innovation without overwhelming your team (or department) members.

CASE SCENARIO FIVE

Many of the existing practices, policies, and procedures in your team (or department) have been around for a long time. In fact, they've been around so long it's difficult to imagine doing things differently. Your team (or department) always purchases the same program to help students. You've always had the same late-work policy. You've always had the same homework procedures. Leading your team (or department) to think about changing these programs (or practices), policies, and procedures will be difficult. You're not sure how to inspire your team (or department) to innovate when members think the status quo is "good enough."

SUBMIT A CASE SCENARIO

Ask teacher leaders to anonymously submit a current scenario that calls for innovation or addresses a barrier to innovation.

The Agree-or-Disagree Line

Invite participants to examine each of the following statements. Allow participants a few minutes to process, and then ask them to stand on the right side of the room if they agree with the statement or the left side of the room if they disagree with the statement. Once participants have chosen their side, open the floor up for discussion by asking, "Why do you agree or disagree with the statement?" The discussion will help participants learn more about the importance of a teacher leader having innovation skills.

» **Statement one:** I find it easy to be innovative.

» **Statement two:** There are no new ideas left in education.

» **Statement three:** We tend to recycle ideas in education, making it challenging to be innovative.

» **Statement four:** I don't want to overshadow someone by coming up with new ideas.

» **Statement five:** Our plate is full—we don't need more new ideas.

» **Statement six:** I'm used to what we do, so it's hard to think about things differently.

» **Statement seven:** I'd rather execute someone's innovative idea than come up with an innovative idea myself.

Strengthen Innovation Activity

This activity allows teacher leaders to tap into their creative and innovative side. First, brainstorm some challenges your school is currently facing as a school leadership team. Some examples include the following.

» Students come late to class.

» Students don't turn in work.

» Students turn work in late.

» Teachers suspend students a lot, so they miss instructional time.

» Students are not engaged in class.

» Teachers refer too many students for interventions.

» Intervention period isn't working.

» Teachers are not enriching students who master the standards because they're focusing too much time on students who did not master the standards.

» Students don't come to class.

After brainstorming, work with participants to select one challenge to resolve in an innovative way. Next, describe what the ideal situation would look like if that challenge did not exist. Paint a picture of the ideal future, maybe five years from now (Eisler, 2021).

Then, work backward to create milestones along the way. What needs to happen four years from now to make your ideal future a reality? What should be your main focus? What does the team need to avoid doing?

Repeat the same process for three years out, two years out, one year out, and the present. By the time they've finished the activity, teacher leaders will have charted a plan for the next five years to make their vision a reality.

Consider using the *"yes and" game* to help with the brainstorming process (Eisler, 2021). This game has participants meet any introduced idea with even more ideas, such as "Yes, and what if we also did this . . . ?" The purpose is quantity of ideas rather than quality, which encourages participants to bring creativity and innovation to the exercise.

Use figure 10.3 to complete this activity.

Timeline	Goal	Innovative Idea to Make It Happen	"Yes and . . ."	"Yes and . . ."
Five Years From Now				
Four Years From Now				
Three Years From Now				
Two Years From Now				
One Year From Now				
Right Now				

FIGURE 10.3: Innovation activity.

*Visit **go.SolutionTree.com/PLCbooks** for a free reproducible of this figure.*

Summary

Innovation is critical to school improvement because continuing to do things the same way every year isn't sufficient to meet students' diverse challenges. Status quo practices cannot result in school improvement. Status quo will result in status quo. To challenge the status quo, teacher leaders must access creativity and innovation. Thinking and brainstorming creative solutions are essential for successfully leading the work of a PLC. Consider how your school leadership team can use the activities in this chapter to plan your professional learning about developing innovation skills.

REPRODUCIBLE

Reflect on Developing Innovation Skills

Pause to reflect on what you've read in this chapter. Use the following prompts to journal about what you learned and next steps you'll take.

Before reading this chapter, how would you have described the relationship between leadership and being innovative?

After reading this chapter and participating in the activities, what have you learned about your (or your teacher leaders') innovation skills?

What do you plan to do to continuously strengthen your (or your teacher leaders') innovation skills?

CHAPTER 11

Developing Decision-Making Skills

*D*ecision making is the essential skill that allows you to choose between two or more options. Decision making is different from problem solving; *problem solving* is about brainstorming solutions you need to identify, evaluate, and review. *Decision making* is about selecting what option provides the best way forward. Regardless of how simple or difficult the choice, decision making itself can be a challenging process.

Decision making is a critical part of every meeting a teacher leader facilitates. Effective meetings include decision making—if there is no decision to make, then the meeting is for sharing information, which can often be done via email. So teacher leaders should be clear every time they lead meetings, they know what decisions need to be made. Meetings aren't the only time teacher leaders are responsible for making decisions, of course. Administrators often call on teacher leaders to make strategic (long-term), tactical (short-term), or operational (day-to-day) decisions on behalf of their team or department.

A specific challenge for teacher leaders in making decisions is they might not believe they have the authority to make them. Clearly communicate how you expect teacher leaders to make decisions to overcome this challenge. Principals can further encourage teacher leaders to develop strong decision-making skills using specific practices, which I discuss in the following section.

In this chapter, I explore practices to help teacher leaders grow decision-making skills. Next, I discuss the PLC connection—specifically to big idea number one (focus on learning). The chapter ends with a series of professional development activities to support teacher leaders to develop strong decision-making skills.

Practices for Developing Decision-Making Skills

Teachers make thousands of decisions each day. Some are conscious decisions, while many are not. What can teacher leaders do to strengthen their decision-making skills to consciously make choices that support learning for *all* students? Consider the following tips to develop strong decision-making skills.

» **Correctly identify the problem:** Decision making often comes in the context of solving a problem. Before making a decision, it's key that teacher leaders understand the nature of the problem. It's easy to jump into making a decision, but if it's based on misunderstanding, it may not be the best decision. Taking the time and care to correctly identify the root of the problem lays the foundation for leaders to make informed decisions.

» **Gather diverse perspectives:** Leaders must carefully consider diverse perspectives rather than one single source. If teacher leaders have only one data point or one source of information on which to base a decision, they're not well informed and could be missing key information. Leaders should commit to surrounding themselves with diverse perspectives and sources of information so they can make a conscious decision based on well-rounded information.

» **Be selective about sources:** On the flip side, leaders can sometimes have *too much* information. Too much information can hinder the decision-making process because so many variables make it difficult to sift through everything to come up with the best possible decision. Again, the key for teacher leaders is to make intentional choices about their sources of data.

» **Take calculated risks:** It can be tempting to stick with the status quo when making decisions. However, staying with what is known and comfortable motivates teacher leaders who make this choice. Encourage teacher leaders to recognize the moments that call for a calculated risk and to be courageous in making the right decision, even when it's uncomfortable.

» **Stand behind decisions:** Teacher leaders sometimes worry about how colleagues will receive their decisions—for example, what their department (or team) will think about the teacher leaders when they make an unpopular decision. Even if a decision doesn't impact them, team members could still judge leaders for it. Therefore, it's important to stand behind whatever decision you make. Understanding teacher leaders must stand behind the decisions they make can also motivate them to carefully evaluate all options before making that final decision.

» **Create a process for reversing a poor decision:** Despite their best efforts, teacher leaders do sometimes make mistakes. When they implement a decision and it becomes clear it wasn't the right decision, teacher leaders need a process for reversing the decision. When decisions are changed quickly from one day to the next, it's disorienting, chaotic, and can cause staff to doubt their leaders. But by having an intentional and thoughtful process for reversing decisions, one that includes thorough communication with staff, teacher leaders have a stronger chance of maintaining trust as they transition to a more aligned decision.

» **Let emotions run their course:** Emotions are messengers, offering important information about the complex tasks administrators have called on teacher leaders to manage each day. However, successful school leaders know teacher leaders must process emotions rather than act on them. Decisions made from a strong emotion rarely align with a leader's values and goals. To process strong emotions, teacher leaders should practice recognizing, naming, and waiting for their emotions to run their course. As teacher leaders allow the emotion to pass and gain clarity, they are well positioned to make an informed decision.

Developing strong decision-making skills is essential for teacher leaders to advance the work of their PLC. Offer teacher leaders support and practice to grow their expertise with this skill.

The PLC Connection: Focus on Learning

As part of ensuring every student achieves at high levels, collaborative teams in a PLC focus their efforts on the four critical questions (DuFour et al., 2024): (1) What do we want all students to learn? (2) How will we know if they've learned it? (3) What do we do when they don't learn it? (4) How will we enrich and extend the learning for students who are proficient?

Discussing each of these questions in collaborative meetings requires teachers to make decisions. It's easier to base those decisions on the path of least resistance or least discomfort, rather than making the hard decisions that truly advance student learning. Let's review some of the decisions the four critical questions of a PLC require teachers to make.

Critical Question One—What Do We Want All Students to Learn?

When teams collaborate to answer this critical question, they must decide their guaranteed and viable curriculum. The team must decide which standards are essential and then make decisions for how to unpack the standards into learning targets. Teacher leaders should not make decisions related to critical question one of the PLC process based on personal preferences or colleagues' opinions. Additionally, teacher leaders should review and tweak these decisions yearly to ensure the guaranteed and viable curriculum is current and helping to advance student learning for all students.

Critical Question Two—How Will We Know If They've Learned It?

Critical question two calls on teachers to make decisions, especially when it comes to assessment. Specifically, collaborative teams decide what kinds of questions will be on the assessment. Members decide whether all questions tie to essential standards and how they will administer the assessment. For example, is the collaborative team going to give an open-book test or take-home test? These are all decisions the team makes together in response to critical question two.

Another big decision with critical question two relates to grading. This area can be challenging for teacher leaders to facilitate because the goal is for teachers to reach consensus and consistency about how to grade assessments. Teacher leaders should ensure that when making these decisions, team members create *consistency across classrooms*; this means that an *A* in one teacher's class equates to an *A* in the other teachers' classes. These decisions impact student learning! While it would be much easier to use the same tests, same questions, and same grading standards year after year, that is not an approach that ensures high achievement for all students.

When deciding which questions should be on the assessment or how teachers grade the assessment, it's helpful to let object questions (rather than preferences or past approaches) guide the process—for example, "Does the question assess the standard?" "Does the rigor of the question match the rigor of the standard?" and so on.

Critical Question Three—What Do We Do When Students Don't Learn It?

Some of the decisions to make using question three might include, Which teacher will reteach material students fail to master? and Which strategies might help teachers reteach this material with more success than the first attempt? Given that some students didn't master the material the first time, teacher leaders must bring problem solving and decision making to the process of figuring out *why* students didn't learn the material, and what teachers should do to ensure students master it during reteaching.

Note that decision making for addressing question three is difficult to do if collaborative teams don't make good decisions in addressing critical questions one and two! Teams must identify and understand essential standards and ensure assessments align to standards if they are to make effective decisions about reteaching and interventions.

Critical Question Four—How Will We Enrich and Extend the Learning for Students Who Are Proficient?

In regard to critical question four, teacher leaders must decide how to extend the learning for students who master essential standards. How should teacher leaders make such decisions? Not by looking for the path of least resistance, assigning busywork, or providing more work on the standards students already mastered. Teachers must base these decisions on a process that ties extensions back to the standards. Additionally, teacher leaders should review the extensions to ensure they produce the desired effect.

For collaborative teams in a PLC, a *focus on learning* means the four critical questions guide their work, which calls them to make many important decisions. Teacher leaders must look for data to guide these decisions, be willing to take risks (rather than stick with the status quo), and monitor their decisions to ensure they achieve the desired outcome. Teacher leaders in a PLC must continuously evaluate whether the decisions they make result in improved learning for all students. That is teacher leaders' whole purpose!

PAUSE TO REFLECT

Pause for a moment to reflect on the following questions.

» What barriers do teacher leaders face when making decisions?

» What are the benefits of teacher leaders making effective decisions?

» What support do teacher leaders need to help them make good decisions?

» How will developing decision-making skills advance the work of your PLC?

Professional Development Activities for Developing Decision-Making Skills

Now that you've explored the importance of decision making and why it's essential for strong teacher leaders, consider professional development activities to help teacher leaders develop decision-making skills.

Self-Assessment for Developing Decision-Making Skills

A self-assessment is a great way for teacher leaders to reflect on their current reality, specifically their strengths and challenges when it comes to decision making. Provide teacher leaders with the self-assessment in figure 11.1, and encourage them to determine specific areas of growth to strengthen their decision-making skills.

Instructions: Read each statement and indicate whether it applies to you consistently, usually, occasionally, or rarely. Next, set goals for improving weak aspects of this skill.	Consistently	Usually	Occasionally	Rarely
I consider all potential solutions before I make my final decision.	☐	☐	☐	☐
I tend to make decisions I know my department or team will support.	☐	☐	☐	☐
I like to get input from my department or team, but I will ultimately make the decision myself.	☐	☐	☐	☐

I dig deeper to find the root cause before making any decision.	☐	☐	☐	☐
I find it hard to make decisions because someone will always be upset with me.	☐	☐	☐	☐
Decisions can be challenging because I know I have to deal with the consequences of every decision I make for my department or team.	☐	☐	☐	☐
I prefer administrators to make the decisions for my department or team.	☐	☐	☐	☐
I feel the need for my administrator's approval before I implement my decisions.	☐	☐	☐	☐

Look back over your answers. Here, set goals that will support you to improve your ability to make decisions.

FIGURE 11.1: Assess your decision-making skills.

*Visit **go.SolutionTree.com/PLCbooks** for a free reproducible of this figure.*

Conversation Starters

Planned conversation starters are a great way to initiate discussions about decision making and allow participants to learn from peers' diverse perspectives.

Use the quotes and discussion questions in figure 11.2 (page 154) as conversation starters. As a school leadership team, share your answers, and participate in a discussion on developing your decision-making skills.

Quotes	Discussion Questions
"The quality of your life is built on the quality of your decisions." —Wesam Fawzi	• How do your decisions impact your life? • How do your decisions impact your department or team? • How can you make high-quality decisions? • Share an example of how a high-quality decision you made impacted you.
"Decision is a sharp knife that cuts clean and straight; indecision, a dull one that hacks and tears and leaves ragged edges behind it." —Gordon Graham	• Why does Graham describe *indecision* this way? • What kinds of situations make you indecisive? • How might your indecision impact your department or team? • How can you avoid indecisiveness?
"You cannot make progress without making decisions." —Jim Rohn	• How does decision making lead to progress? • Has avoiding decisions kept you from making progress in your department or team? How? • What progress has your department or team made in the last five years? How has decision making been a part of that progress? • Do you perpetuate the status quo or initiate change? How do you make those decisions?
"Life is filled with difficult decisions, and winners are those who make them." —Dan Brown	• What difficult decisions are you currently facing? • What consequences might you experience if you avoid making difficult decisions? • What does this quote mean about being "winners"? • What makes a decision difficult?
"Decision making is power. Most people don't have the guts to make the 'tough decision' because they want to make the 'right decision' and so they make 'no decision.'" —Yama Mubtaker	• As a teacher leader, do you feel that you have the power to make decisions? Why or why not? • What does "decision making is power" mean? • How do you develop "the guts" to make the tough decisions? • How are "tough" decisions different from "right" decisions?
"There is a big difference between motion and action. Just because you get out of bed doesn't mean you are making progress. Taking action requires decisiveness, dedication, and clear direction." —Farshad Asl	• How are decisions and actions related? • Can you make a decision without action? Why or why not? • What kinds of actions should you take after making a decision? • What are some reasons leaders may not take action after making a decision?

"Don't mourn over your bad decisions. Just start overcoming them with good ones." —Joyce Meyer	• Why would a leader "mourn over" a bad decision? • What is a bad decision you've made in the past? What made it bad? • Why is it difficult to overcome bad decisions? • How do you overcome a bad decision?

FIGURE 11.2: Let's talk about decision making conversation starters.

*Visit **go.SolutionTree.com/PLCbooks** for a free reproducible of this figure.*

Case Scenarios

Use any of the following case scenarios to facilitate a discussion with teacher leaders about the importance of decision making in their role. After reading the case scenario, discuss how teacher leaders should make a decision in that situation, especially after receiving advice from colleagues to leave the situation alone. As a school leader, do you address the situation or do you leave it alone?

CASE SCENARIO ONE

Teachers on your team are having challenges collaborating with one another. They have no problem meeting and going through an agenda, but the conversations are very superficial and compliant. However, the dynamics of this team are interesting. One teacher is good friends with a board member and another teacher is married to a principal in the district. The advice you receive is to leave the situation alone.

CASE SCENARIO TWO

Several parents complain to you about one of your colleagues in your department (or team). The parents share similar issues with this colleague, who they say is mean, yells at students, and does not seem to enjoy teaching. You have witnessed these behaviors yourself; however, you know this teacher is going through a bad divorce and has not always been like this. The teacher is struggling in his personal life. The advice you receive is to leave the situation alone and it will all be fine once the teacher gets "back to himself."

CASE SCENARIO THREE

You've noticed when walking the hallways of your department (or grade-level) area there is no student work displayed, or when it is, it is very outdated. There are no pictures; the walls are bare. You know the teachers each have so much on their plate that if you ask them to take on correcting this, they will be unhappy. The teachers' classrooms look great—it's just the hallways that need some attention. The advice you receive is to leave the situation alone because, in the big scheme of things, appearance of hallways is not that important.

CASE SCENARIO FOUR

After reviewing student-discipline data, your department (or team) seems to have the most office referrals. You want to bring this up with your teachers but know it will be difficult for them to hear. The number of referrals was brought up a few months ago, and the teachers did not receive that message well. You also are aware that student behaviors have been particularly challenging this year. The advice you receive is to leave the situation alone because once these students leave, next year will be better.

CASE SCENARIO FIVE

Teachers are doing a good job providing interventions to students based on their specific targeted skills; however, enrichments are lacking. Students who demonstrate mastery of the essential standards are usually given more of the same work, tasked with completing worksheets, or told to read. You also know that because the teachers have been working so hard to get their interventions right, if you ask them to do one more thing, they will lose their momentum. The advice you receive is to leave the situation alone. The teachers have made some huge accomplishments worth celebrating.

SUBMIT A CASE SCENARIO

Ask teacher leaders to anonymously submit a current scenario outlining a challenge they need to resolve.

The Agree-or-Disagree Line

Invite participants to examine each of the following statements. Allow participants a few minutes to process, and then ask them to stand on the right side of the room if they agree with the statement or the left side of the room if they disagree with the statement. Once participants have chosen their side, open the floor up for discussion by asking, "Why do you agree or disagree with the statement?" The discussion will help participants learn more about the importance of a teacher leader having decision-making skills.

> » **Statement one:** Decision making always involves multiple steps.

> » **Statement two:** It's always best to have multiple solutions to consider before making a decision.

» **Statement three:** The hardest part about decision making is implementing the decision with my department (or team).

» **Statement four:** Making decisions is difficult because I have to deal with the consequences.

» **Statement five:** I'd much rather my administrator make the decisions, and I'll do the hard part of communicating the decision to my department (or team).

» **Statement six:** I love the opportunity to make decisions for my department (or team) as a teacher leader.

» **Statement seven:** Sometimes I base my decisions on intuition or a gut feeling.

Decision-Making Activity

Begin by brainstorming decisions your department or team needs to make. When suggesting potential decisions, participants should keep in mind two dimensions: (1) the effort needed to execute the decision, and (2) the impact the decision will have on the department or team.

When looking at the effort needed while you're brainstorming decisions, think about the time and resources teacher leaders require to implement the decision. Then, discuss the rating for this particular dimension for each potential decision. Review each decision and determine whether that decision is high effort or low effort.

When looking at the potential impact, think about the consequence each decision will have on student achievement. Will the decision significantly impact student achievement or not? Again, review each decision, and determine whether each will have a high impact or low impact on student achievement.

Using chart paper, create a four-quadrant graph, similar to the one in figure 11.3 (page 158). Explain each of the four quadrants as follows.

» **Low Effort/Low Impact:** Discuss how these decisions will take low effort but will also have a low impact on student achievement. These are decisions teacher leaders may want to consider implementing as tasks.

» **Low Effort/High Impact:** Discuss how these decisions will take low effort but will have a high impact on student achievement. These are the decisions teacher leaders probably want to execute right away!

» **High Effort/Low Impact:** Discuss how these decisions will take high effort but will have a low impact on student achievement. These are the decisions teacher leaders might want to implement later.

» **High Effort/High Impact:** Discuss how these decisions will take high effort but will have a high impact on student achievement. These are the decisions teacher leaders should execute with considerable front-end planning.

Impact	Low Effort/High Impact	High Effort/High Impact
	Low Effort/Low Impact	High Effort/Low Impact
	Effort	

FIGURE 11.3: Decision-making activity.

Give participants sticky dots or notes and ask them to label each decision as high effort or low effort, and then as high impact or low impact, and instruct them to place each decision on the graph.

Summary

It is important for leaders to make decisions, but effective and efficient decision making is a learned skill. Teacher leaders may be tempted to leave decision making to others, but that approach will not advance the work of the PLC or lead to high achievement for all students. With dedication, practice, and the principal's support, teacher leaders can grow their ability to make informed decisions, gain buy-in from colleagues, and plan successful implementation. Consider how your school leadership team can use the activities in this chapter to plan your professional learning about growing decision-making skills.

Reflect on Developing Decision-Making Skills

Pause to reflect on what you've read in this chapter. Use the following prompts to journal about what you learned and next steps you'll take.

Before reading this chapter, how would you have described the relationship between leadership and decision making?

After reading this chapter and participating in the activities, what have you learned about your (or your teacher leaders') decision-making skills?

What do you plan to do to continuously strengthen your (or your teacher leaders') decision-making skills?

CHAPTER 12

Developing Problem-Solving Skills

All schools have problems waiting for educators to solve. The difference between a PLC school and a traditional school is that a PLC school is filled with teacher leaders who are problem solvers. In traditional schools, teachers typically wait for school administrators to solve problems as they arise, but in a PLC school, the school administrators train teacher leaders to be problem solvers and participate in the process.

Catherine Cote (2023), marketing coordinator at Harvard Business School Online, writes, "*Problem-solving* is the process of systematically removing barriers that prevent you or others from reaching goals." Why is problem solving a key skill for teacher leaders? Because if they are deeply committed to achieving their PLC's mission and vision, unresolved problems will prevent them from making progress. Problem solving helps teacher leaders stay focused on achieving their school's goals.

In this chapter, I explore five steps to help teacher leaders solve problems. Next, I discuss the PLC connection—specifically to big idea number three (a results orientation). The chapter ends with a series of professional development activities to support teacher leaders to develop strong problem-solving skills.

Problem Solving in Five Steps

Leaders face problems in all industries, but leaders cannot be the only ones responsible for solving them. Cote (2023) writes about problem solving as a shared endeavor: "As a leader, it's rarely your responsibility to solve a problem single-handedly, so it's crucial to know how to empower employees to work together to find the best solution."

The challenge of course is *how*. How do you cultivate more problem solvers in your building? First, spend some time with teacher leaders to explain what the skill of problem solving looks like in practice. In essence, a problem is an obstacle standing in the way of achieving your school's mission, vision, and goals. *Problem solving* is both about identifying existing problems in your department or grade level *and* being committed to finding and implementing appropriate solutions to solve those problems.

Problem solving is also about being proactive. Executive, entrepreneur, and senior adviser Glenn Llopis (2013) writes, "As leaders, the goal is to minimize the occurrence of problems—which means we must be courageous enough to tackle them head-on before circumstances force our hand." For example, educators know every school year they will have parents upset with them. What can educators do to proactively prepare for upset parents? One solution is to use a Pareto chart, a problem-solving tool well-suited to the common problems educators face (American Society for Quality [ASQ], n.d.). A *Pareto chart* organizes data from greatest to least, providing a powerful visualization of challenges from most to least significant. Figure 12.1 is a sample Pareto chart illustrating common parent complaints. The graph identifies the number of parent complaints teachers received over the course of a month, quarter, semester, and school year on the *y*-axis and the type of complaints on the *x*-axis. The leadership team that compiled this graph might use the data to start a conversation about how they will address these four common parent complaints.

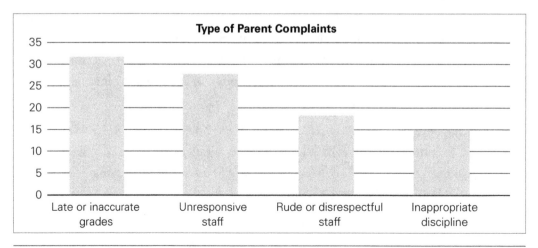

FIGURE 12.1: Sample Pareto chart.

A Pareto chart offers leadership teams a great tool for identifying the frequency or severity of problems to prioritize their focus and effort.

Ultimately, problem solving should help advance your school's mission, vision, and goals—which is the fundamental reason educators engage in the work of a PLC. Josh Axe (2023), an expert on mindset and leadership, writes about problem solving in organizations:

> An effective organization will have systems and processes in place to reach their goals and solve problems. If a company has team members and leaders who have poor problem-solving skills, that means they're *ineffective at one of the core functions* of a business.

Axe (2023) goes on to identify a five-step problem-solving process: (1) define the problem, (2) brainstorm possible solutions, (3) research several options, (4) select a solution, and (5) develop an action plan. The following sections look at each of these steps in more detail.

Define the Problem

Identifying the problem is an important first step. Sometimes you have an idea of the potential obstacles or challenges but don't take the time to determine their cause. The more specific you can be when identifying the problem, the higher your chance of successfully solving it. Axe (2023) explains: "Sometimes the surface issue isn't what you need to address. Just like an earthquake, organizational issues have an epicenter—complete with shockwaves that negatively impact the business." When defining the problem, try to get to the root cause of the problem rather than treat the symptoms.

Another problem-solving tool educators may find helpful is the *5 Whys* method Toyota Industries founder Sakichi Toyoda developed in the 1930s (as cited in Mind Tools Content Team, n.d.). This method involves asking *why* repeatedly to get to the root cause of the problem. So when a problem exists, ask, "Why did this happen?" Once you receive an answer, ask why again. After that answer, ask why again. Do this a total of five times. By the fifth time, you will have peeled back all the layers of the problem to get to the root cause—which you can now think about how to solve. Figure 12.2 (page 164) illustrates what this method might look like when educators are seeking solutions to student behavior problems.

Problem: Student Behavior

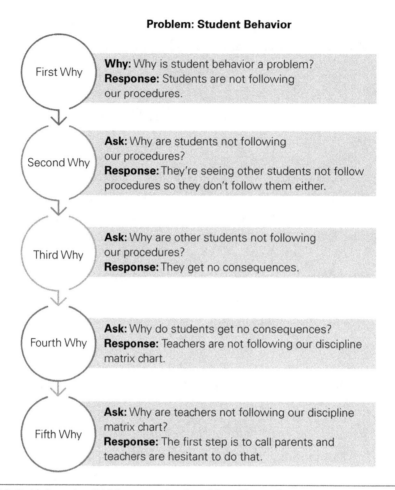

First Why

Why: Why is student behavior a problem?
Response: Students are not following our procedures.

Second Why

Ask: Why are students not following our procedures?
Response: They're seeing other students not follow procedures so they don't follow them either.

Third Why

Ask: Why are other students not following our procedures?
Response: They get no consequences.

Fourth Why

Ask: Why do students get no consequences?
Response: Teachers are not following our discipline matrix chart.

Fifth Why

Ask: Why are teachers not following our discipline matrix chart?
Response: The first step is to call parents and teachers are hesitant to do that.

FIGURE 12.2: Using the 5 Whys method to identify and resolve a student behavior problem.

Brainstorm Possible Solutions

Once you identify the problem, begin brainstorming solutions. Problems are not identical, so each problem will need a brainstorming session to find a customized solution. In other words, there's no one-size-fits-all solution to every problem. This is where you get to be creative! Jot down as many different solutions that come to mind for the problem you identify. Involve colleagues in your department or grade level to help with brainstorming. Remember you're just making a running list of all the possible solutions. All ideas are welcome during this step of problem solving.

Research Several Options

Review the ideas you and others generate in the brainstorming phase to identify the two or three most seemingly effective solutions. Once you narrow down the choice, begin researching the pros and cons for each solution. Involve colleagues to get their input, look at any related data, speak to educators in other schools who may have implemented any of those solutions, and so on. Collaborating during this process will be more productive than working in isolation. For this step, gain as much knowledge as possible for each potential solution to help prepare you for selecting the best solution.

Select a Solution

Now you're ready to select the solution you think will best solve the problem. After you identify the pros and cons of each solution, it's time to evaluate those pros and cons to select the best choice. When selecting your solution, consider the following questions.

» Which solution will best advance our school's mission statement?

» Which solution will enable us to work through the pitfalls in the implementation phase?

» Which solution will create the fewest problems?

Develop an Action Plan

Now think about how you will implement the solution. During this implementation step, consider the who, what, how, when, and where of rolling out the solution. Do your best to think through every aspect of the implementation to ensure the solution's success and monitor the outcome to ensure you're achieving the expected results.

The PLC Connection: A Results Orientation

Data are essential to PLCs. Data inform teams of what is going well and what is not. In essence, examining your data is the prerequisite to problem solving. Through examining data effectively, teams identify the problems and then discuss potential solutions. Critical questions number three (What do we do when they don't learn it?) and four (How will we enrich and extend the learning for students who are proficient?) of the PLC process ask you to identify and solve problems.

Think about the many conversations collaborative teams have about critical question number three of the PLC process. These discussions center on what barriers prevent students from learning the essential standards, but most importantly, how to remove those barriers. What can collaborative teams do differently to ensure students master essential standards? If teachers don't change their practice or do anything different, then the results will be the same—they will fail in their mission to ensure learning for *all* students. What will your team do differently to ensure *all* students learn at high levels?

Teachers need the same level of problem solving to address critical question four of the PLC process. There will always be some students who do learn the essential standards and are ready to extend their learning. What is the plan for them? When it comes to planning enrichments and extensions, you and your team or department members will be engaging in problem solving. What kinds of enrichments or extensions will your team provide that aren't just busywork or more of the same work?

Being results oriented in a PLC is all about using data to improve practice. What problems do the data show? In a PLC, data should drive the discussions about whatever problems your collaborative teams are addressing. As your team implements solutions, review new data to gauge whether the solutions are working. Use the problem-solving steps (see page 162) in this chapter regularly as you and your team problem solve to push forward the work of your PLC. Collaborative teams don't wait for someone to come in to solve the problems for them; the PLC process calls for teacher-driven work within teacher-led collaborative teams. This works best when teacher leaders embody strong problem-solving skills.

PAUSE TO REFLECT

Pause for a moment to reflect on the following questions.

- » Why is a school filled with problem solvers more likely to be successful?
- » How can you support your teacher leaders to become strong problem solvers?
- » How and when can you use the 5 Whys method or Pareto chart?
- » How will developing problem-solving skills advance the work of your PLC?

Professional Development Activities for Problem Solving

Now that you've explored the importance of problem solving for teacher leaders, consider professional development activities to help teacher leaders develop problem-solving skills.

Self-Assessment for Problem-Solving Skills

A self-assessment is a great way for teacher leaders to reflect on their current reality, specifically their strengths and challenges when it comes to problem solving. Provide teacher leaders the self-assessment in figure 12.3 and encourage them to determine specific areas of growth.

Instructions: Read each statement and indicate whether it applies to you consistently, usually, occasionally, or rarely. Next, set goals for improving weak aspects of this skill.				
	Consistently	**Usually**	**Occasionally**	**Rarely**
I have an inquisitive nature and always look for problems to solve.	☐	☐	☐	☐
I take initiative to predict problems before they arise so I can solve them proactively.	☐	☐	☐	☐
I collaborate with others to find solutions to problems.	☐	☐	☐	☐
I take ownership of problems and actively work to solve them instead of waiting for someone else to solve them.	☐	☐	☐	☐
I gather all necessary facts and information before deciding on a solution to a problem.	☐	☐	☐	☐
I seek others to help brainstorm multiple solutions for problems.	☐	☐	☐	☐
I break down problems so I can accurately analyze them.	☐	☐	☐	☐
When faced with high-pressure problems, I always keep a cool head so I can solve them effectively and efficiently.	☐	☐	☐	☐
I am always decisive and assertive when it comes to the solutions.	☐	☐	☐	☐
I actively evaluate the solutions and make changes when needed.	☐	☐	☐	☐
Look back over your answers. Here, set goals that will support you to improve your problem-solving skills.				

FIGURE 12.3: Assess your problem-solving skills.

*Visit **go.SolutionTree.com/PLCbooks** for a free reproducible of this figure.*

Conversation Starters

Planned conversation starters are a great way to initiate discussions and allow participants to learn from peers' diverse perspectives.

Use the quotes and discussion questions in figure 12.4 as conversation starters. As a school leadership team, share your answers, and participate in a discussion on developing your problem-solving skills.

Quotes	Discussion Questions
"One of the true tests of leadership is the ability to recognize a problem before it becomes an emergency." —Arnold Glasow	• What problems do you anticipate in your department or grade level next year? How can you prepare yourself as a leader to solve them? • How can you try to predict problems in your department or grade level before they become emergencies? • How would you rate your ability to forecast problems in your department or grade level? • What is your biggest challenge when it comes to predicting problems in your department or grade level?
"Problems are nothing but wake-up calls for creativity." —Gerhard Gschwandtner	• How are problem solving and creativity related? • How can you tap into your creativity to strengthen your problem-solving skills? • Give an example of the most creative way you solved a problem in your department or grade level. • What is the most challenging problem in your school? Think of a creative way to solve it.
"Sometimes the easiest way to solve a problem is to stop participating in the problem." —Jonathan Mead	• How can participating in the problem make the problem worse? • Why do educators participate in problems rather than solve them? • What skills would you like to strengthen so you can avoid being a part of the problem in your department or grade level? • How can you encourage the teachers in your department or grade level to be part of the solution rather than the problem?
"A problem well stated is a problem half solved." —Charles Kettering	• How does communication play a big part in problem solving? • Reflect on how problems are currently communicated in your department or grade level. How can you improve communication? • Think of a current problem in your department or grade level. What would be effective and ineffective ways to state that problem?

"There are only two ways to solve a problem: stop dwelling, and start doing." —Emily Uraih	• What does "stop dwelling" mean to you as a teacher leader? • What does "start doing" mean to you as a teacher leader? • How do you encourage the teachers in your department or grade level to "stop dwelling, and start doing"? • What do you have a difficult time with when problem solving in your department or grade level?
"A problem is a chance for you to do your best." —Duke Ellington	• How can you use problems to shine as a teacher leader? • What problem would you be proudest to solve? • How can problem solving strengthen your skill set both professionally and personally? • "To do your best," how can you rely less on school administrators to solve problems in your department or grade level?
"The important thing about a problem is not the solution, but the strength we gain in finding a solution." —Seneca	• What strengths can you gain by problem solving? • What benefits do you see from problem solving in collaboration with the teachers in your department or grade level? • How can you put a positive spin on problems in your department or grade level so you can appreciate the strengths that will come from the problem-solving process? • How can you celebrate when your department or grade level solves problems?

FIGURE 12.4: Let's talk about problem solving conversation starters.

*Visit **go.SolutionTree.com/PLCbooks** for a free reproducible of this figure.*

Case Scenarios

Use any of the following case scenarios to facilitate a discussion with teacher leaders about problem solving. After reading the case scenario, discuss how drawing on problem-solving skills will help resolve the situation.

CASE SCENARIO ONE

Teachers in your department (or grade level) have been talking a lot lately about how much student behavior has changed for the worse. Students don't seem to take any of the rules seriously and they seem to have no respect for authority.

CASE SCENARIO TWO

Morale in your department (or grade level) seems to be at an all-time low. Teachers are exhausted, they don't have adequate time to meet their many responsibilities, and they feel their leaders do not appreciate them.

CASE SCENARIO THREE

Teachers are not taking their collaborative meetings seriously. They feel like the meetings are just a waste of time because they would much rather be working independently in their classrooms to finish their planning or grading for the week.

CASE SCENARIO FOUR

You notice the hallways in your department (or grade level) are not very visually appealing. There are some bulletin boards, but the materials on them are not very neatly displayed.

CASE SCENARIO FIVE

The administrators just implemented a new process regarding how teachers will dismiss students for buses at the end of the school day. Teachers in your department (or grade level) don't feel the new dismissal process is working. They are seeing more issues with this new process than they did with the old process.

SUBMIT A CASE SCENARIO

Ask teacher leaders to anonymously submit a current problem they have in their department (or grade level). Use some of those problems as the case scenarios.

The Agree-or-Disagree Line

Invite participants to examine each of the following statements. Allow participants a few minutes to process, and then ask them to stand on the right side of the room if they agree with the statement or the left side of the room if they disagree with the statement. Once participants have chosen their side, open the floor up for discussion by asking, "Why do you agree or disagree with the statement?" The discussion will help participants learn more about the importance of a teacher leader having problem-solving skills.

>> **Statement one:** Problem solving is hard because I don't always know what I'm allowed to do or not allowed to do to solve the problem.

>> **Statement two:** I could quickly solve problems if I am totally in charge.

>> **Statement three:** Solving problems is difficult because I know not everyone in my department (or grade level) is going to like or implement the solution.

>> **Statement four:** I don't have the authority to enforce the solutions to the problems I might solve.

» **Statement five:** I'm hesitant to solve problems because teachers in my department (or grade level) will think I'm trying to be an administrator.

» **Statement six:** Sometimes I don't know which problems I should solve and which problems administrators should solve.

» **Statement seven:** I don't know how to predict problems, so it's hard for me to proactively solve problems.

Problem-Solving Activity

This activity provides an opportunity for teacher leaders to solve problems in their department or grade level. Teacher leaders each outline a current problem in their department or grade level. This problem relates to instruction, operations, climate, personnel, or anything else teacher leaders believe is relevant. After explaining the problem, teacher leaders each propose one or two solutions that could help minimize or solve the problem. Teacher leaders each present their proposal to the whole leadership team to solicit feedback on their solutions. After garnering feedback, teacher leaders each update their solutions. Then, they implement the solutions. After a specified period of time, teacher leaders each present the results of their solution to the leadership team. The team discusses whether the solution worked and if something else is needed to solve the problem. Teams can use the template in figure 12.5 to complete the activity.

Teacher Leader Name:	
Problem Is Related To: • Instruction • Personnel • Operations • Other • Climate	
Describe a current problem in your department or grade level:	
Describe your proposed solution:	
Note feedback you receive from colleagues:	
Describe revisions you've made to your solution based on colleagues' feedback:	
Describe the results you witnessed after implementing the solution:	

FIGURE 12.5: Teacher leader problem-solving activity.

*Visit **go.SolutionTree.com/PLCbooks** for a free reproducible of this figure.*

Summary

Problem solving is a critical skill teacher leaders need to develop and strengthen to help advance their school's mission and vision. Just like any leader, teacher leaders also face problems in their departments or teams. However, principals must provide teacher leaders the right tools and support for them to become effective problem solvers. Consider how your school leadership team can use the activities in this chapter to plan your professional learning about problem solving.

Reflect on Developing Problem-Solving Skills

Pause to reflect on what you've read in this chapter. Use the following prompts to journal about what you learned and next steps you'll take.

Before reading this chapter, how would you have described the relationship between leadership and problem solving?

After reading this chapter and participating in the activities, what have you learned about your (or your teacher leaders') problem-solving skills?

What do you plan to do to continuously strengthen your (or your teacher leaders') problem-solving skills?

CHAPTER 13

Developing Communication Skills

Communication sounds like a no-brainer skill. You could be thinking, "Why do we need to train teacher leaders on how to communicate? Educators communicate all the time!" Yes, but communication is so much more than the words you use. Communication is *everything*. *Communication* is about what you say and don't say, how you say it, when you say it, and why you say it. Communication is complex, so it's no wonder so many challenges stem from either too much communication, a lack of communication, or just simply, miscommunication.

Communication can be a difficult skill to intentionally develop because it is something educators do all the time. Teacher leaders may feel they don't need to improve a facet of their lives they use every day. However, not all communication is equal. Author and columnist Carmine Gallo (2022) points out that successful communication is an art form: "Leaders who reach the top do not simply pay lip service to the importance of effective communication. Instead, they study the art in all its forms—writing, speaking, presenting—and constantly strive to improve on those skills." Teacher leaders who wish to support their PLC to reach its full potential must master the art of effective communication.

In this chapter, I explore practices to help teacher leaders develop strong communication skills. Next, I discuss the PLC connection—specifically to big idea number two (collaborative culture and collective responsibility). The chapter ends with a series of professional development activities to support teacher leaders to develop effective communication skills.

Practices for Developing Communication Skills

There is no doubt that effective communication in schools is essential for success. Leadership coach Patrick Bosworth (n.d.) discusses the four powerful benefits of effective communication in the workplace.

1. **Effective communication mitigates conflict:** How much conflict you experience comes down to *misunderstandings or feeling misunderstood* (that is, not understanding how others communicate or disregarding others' emotional needs).

2. **Effective communication increases employee engagement:** Communication is about connecting with others. Effective communication allows you to better understand what motivates and inspires your teachers, and their talents and skills, which helps cultivate their skill set to align to your school's mission, vision, and goals.

3. **Effective communication creates better relationships:** With effective communication, you will have stronger and more positive relationships with your stakeholders. You're able to resolve conflicts, understand needs, and present information in a way that others will better receive it.

4. **Effective communication results in a more productive workforce:** Effective communication allows you to create a safe working environment, where teachers can think creatively and express their ideas. It can also help you influence teachers in the school to try different things or achieve more buy-in.

Imagine how accessing these benefits would empower your teacher leaders and improve your PLC! So, what can teacher leaders do to strengthen their communication skills? Consider the following suggestions (Moore, 2019).

» **Practice perceiving others' emotional state:** Being aware of others' emotions is critical to communication. You need to be able to read someone's mood or even body language. Is now a good time to communicate the message, or should you wait until later when the person might receive it better? Remember the purpose of the message you're communicating; you want to achieve that purpose. To achieve that purpose, keep in mind how the other person will take your message. Sometimes it's better to wait to achieve the purpose of your communication. Learn to read other people's emotions to help you determine this timing.

» **Become self-aware:** Be aware of your own body language. What are your nonverbal cues communicating? *Body language* not only refers to your gestures or posture but also the tone of your voice and facial expression—all the things you do without words are forms of communication. Being aware of this helps ensure your nonverbal body language communicates your meaning as well (as opposed to contradicting it). It's easy to show your frustration or anger through your body language, but that can derail the message you are trying to communicate. It's not just about the verbal communication but also the nonverbal communication.

» **Make sure communication is mutual:** Communication goes both ways. Communication isn't always about you sending a message to others; it's about having others send a message to you as well. Think about the times when during a meeting, one person dominates while others sit quietly. Effective communication is about giving everyone an opportunity to engage in those conversations. Every time you engage in communication, be cognizant of how much time you give the other person to communicate. Remember communication is not just about you communicating your message.

» **Be a good listener:** To give others a chance to engage, you must actively listen to what they are communicating. "Talking is essentially a form of content delivery, and it's not really communication unless we listen" (Moore, 2019). *Active listening* means you are fully engaged with the person who is communicating with you. You are asking appropriate questions, restating what the person said to ensure understanding, and are not distracted, interrupting, or talking over the person. Communication is actually more about listening than it is talking.

» **Don't get defensive:** It's hard to hear others make negative comments about you, but getting defensive is not the answer! Becoming defensive perpetuates conflict and shuts down productive communication. Instead, listen and acknowledge. Researcher Courtney Ackerman (2019) advises, "Imagine you are a fog. When someone throws a stone at you, you absorb that stone without throwing the stone back." Figure 13.1 (page 178) shows some examples.

When Someone Says . . .	You Respond With . . .
"You just don't understand."	"You're right. I don't understand."
"You are lazy."	"I can be lazy sometimes."
"You are always late."	"I am sometimes late."
"You're not getting it."	"You're right. I'm not getting it."

Source: Adapted from Ackerman, 2019.

FIGURE 13.1: Examples of non-defensive communication.

The responses in figure 13.1 apply in situations where the criticism is accurate. Absorbing criticism doesn't mean being a doormat or agreeing with inaccurate statements. Stay present during challenging conversations and pause as needed to discern the best response. If a criticism is untrue, simply state the truth. The more you can practice listening, absorbing criticism, and simply stating the truth without taking criticism personally, the more you will "disarm the person criticizing you" (Ackerman, 2019). Notice how absorbing the criticism or simply stating the truth defuses conflict instead of perpetuating it. This is the path to productive communication. Communication is a two-way street. It is just as much about listening and receiving messages from others as it is about talking and relaying messages to others.

The PLC Connection: Collaborative Culture and Collective Responsibility

Every leadership skill needed in a PLC will always involve effective communication skills. Whether teacher leaders are solving a problem, making a decision, having a tough conversation, or trying to change something in their PLC, all require communication. Communication can quickly either strengthen or weaken your collaborative team. What are some of the hallmarks of communication that strengthen rather than weaken a team?

First, approach tough conversations in a respectful manner. This doesn't mean you avoid conflict, but rather navigate it by giving others the benefit of the doubt and seeking compromise where possible. Debates and disagreements will arise, but leaders should ensure their words demonstrate professionalism. When a colleague says something rash or disparaging in the heat of the moment, those words can have a lasting effect on their teammates.

There will be conflict in your collaborative team. You could handle that conflict *overtly*, which could result in a lot of angry words being said, or *covertly*, which could result in no words being said. Everyone pretends to go along with the collaboration, but no one wants to talk about the issues. Moments like this call on leaders to draw on their ability to have *courageous conversations* (see chapter 5, page 63). Leaders should be bold enough to have tough conversations, sharing their concerns with honesty and confidence in themselves and their teammates.

Another hallmark of successful communication is *clarity*. Too many or not enough words lead to confusion. Confusion then leads to teams not executing the work the way it was originally intended or team members ignoring you. Executive coach and author Melody Wilding (2020) explains why this happens: "People get impatient when they have to work mental overtime to grasp what you're saying." Leaders should bring *self-awareness* to their communication, striving to check their ego and focus on clearly stating the problem and the desired solution during moments of conflict. Take out all the unnecessary words and phrases, and stick to the goals you need to accomplish during contentious conversations and meetings.

Body language is a primary source of communication teacher leaders should be conscious of during meetings and conversations. For example, how team members behave during collaborative meetings communicates a message. If teacher leaders spend most of the interaction on their phone or staring off into space, it suggests disinterest or distraction, which is not conducive to effective communication.

Teacher leaders should practice reflecting on their communication skills. After every challenging conversation, meeting, or interaction, take five minutes to review. How did your communication skills affect the interaction? Did you avoid being defensive? Did you clearly state your needs and expectations? Were you aware of participants' body language and emotional state? Did the conversation produce the desired outcome? What will you try differently next time? Effective communication is essential for teacher leaders to successfully lead colleagues in a PLC, and self-reflection is a powerful practice for growing this skill over time.

PAUSE TO REFLECT

Pause for a moment to reflect on the following questions.

» How can communication be challenging for teacher leaders?

» How does communication intersect with other leadership skills?

» Which practices most strongly resonate with you as being helpful for developing teacher leaders' communication skills?

» How will developing communication skills advance the work of your PLC?

Professional Development Activities for Strengthening Communication Skills

Now that you've explored the importance of strong communication and why it's essential for strong teacher leaders, consider professional development activities to help teacher leaders develop their communication skills.

Self-Assessment for Communication Skills

A self-assessment is a great way for teacher leaders to reflect on their current reality, specifically their strengths and challenges with communication. Provide teacher leaders with the self-assessment in figure 13.2 and encourage them to determine specific areas for growth.

Instructions: Read each statement and indicate whether it applies to you consistently, usually, occasionally, or rarely. Next, set goals for improving weak aspects of this skill.				
	Consistently	**Usually**	**Occasionally**	**Rarely**
I listen without interrupting.	☐	☐	☐	☐
I pay attention to my body language because I know it's a form of communication.	☐	☐	☐	☐
I always think before I speak.	☐	☐	☐	☐
I communicate clearly, efficiently, and effectively.	☐	☐	☐	☐
I try to be aware and try to understand people's moods and emotions before I communicate anything.	☐	☐	☐	☐
I need to understand my emotional awareness before I communicate. (For example, should I be communicating when I'm upset or angry?)	☐	☐	☐	☐
I set aside all distractions so I can actively listen.	☐	☐	☐	☐
Look back over your answers. Here, set goals that will support you to improve your communication skills.				

FIGURE 13.2: Assess your communication skills.

*Visit **go.SolutionTree.com/PLCbooks** for a free reproducible of this figure.*

Conversation Starters

Planned conversation starters are a great way to initiate discussions about communication skills and allow participants to learn from peers' diverse perspectives.

Use the quotes and discussion questions in figure 13.3 as conversation starters. As a school leadership team, share your answers, and participate in a discussion about developing your communication skills.

Quotes	Discussion Questions
"We have two ears and one mouth so that we can listen twice as much as we speak." —Epictetus	• How much do you listen in comparison to how much you talk? • How can you monitor that ratio? • If you realize you need to listen more, how do you do that? • What prevents you from talking less and listening more?
"The single biggest problem in communication is the illusion that it has taken place." —George Bernard Shaw	• What does it mean to say someone is under "the illusion that it [communication] has taken place"? • How can this quote explain the concept of miscommunication? • What can you do to ensure you're not under a false impression that you've communicated something important to a colleague? • Do you agree that having a false impression that you have communicated something is the biggest problem with communication? Why or why not?
"The most important thing in communication is hearing what isn't said." —Peter Drucker	• What are some examples of "what isn't said" (think about nonverbal communication)? • What impact does nonverbal communication have on verbal communication? • Why do people sometimes fail to pay attention to nonverbal communication? • How can you become more aware of nonverbal communication? Why would this awareness be helpful?
"Communication is about being effective, not always about being proper." —Bo Bennett	• What does *"proper" communication* mean, and how is it different from effective communication? • Do you agree that communication must be effective—regardless of it being proper? Why or why not? • Can communication be both proper and effective? Why or why not? • How do you ensure effective communication as a teacher leader?

FIGURE 13.3: Let's talk about communication conversation starters. continued ▶

Quotes	Discussion Questions
"We never listen when we are eager to speak." —Francois de la Rochefoucauld	• Why are people always so "eager to speak" instead of listen? • What prevents people from listening well? • What kinds of things go on in your mind when you're not actively listening to others? • What steps can you take to be an active listener?
"Effective communication is 20% what you know and 80% how you feel about what you know." —Jim Rohn	• What do feelings have to do with communication? • Do you agree with the percentage values in this quote? Why or why not? • Describe a time you communicated while you were experiencing a strong emotion. How did it go? • What is the relationship between "what you know" and "how you feel about what you know"?
"Good communication is the bridge between confusion and clarity." —Nat Turner	• How can communication lead to confusion? • How can communication lead to clarity? • Describe a time your communication caused confusion. Why or how did this happen? • What steps can you take to ensure your communication results in clarity?

*Visit **go.SolutionTree.com/PLCbooks** for a free reproducible of this figure.*

Case Scenarios

Use any of the following case scenarios to facilitate a discussion with teacher leaders about communication. After reading the case scenario, encourage participants to share how they would ensure effective and efficient communication.

CASE SCENARIO ONE

A teacher in your department (or team) comes to you about a parent email. This parent wrote an email to the teacher because she's terribly upset with him. The parent explains how she had no idea her daughter was failing his class. Her daughter is passing all her other classes, but not this one. Her daughter does not like the way he teaches, and the parent also writes about how it takes the teacher "forever" to return assignments, so her daughter never really knows how she's doing in his class. Her daughter also feels like the teacher doesn't like her because he tends to ignore her every time she raises her hand to answer a question.

CASE SCENARIO TWO

A teacher in your department (or team) is sitting in a district-provided training, and she looks incredibly bored. At one point, the teacher almost dozes off, so she begins to doodle. She is staring down at her paper to avoid making eye contact with anyone, so it looks like she's taking notes. She is sitting slouched down as well because she is so disinterested in this training. Then the teacher picks up and stays on her phone for the majority of the training.

CASE SCENARIO THREE

Teachers in your department (or team) are experiencing some challenges with students in their classroom. The teachers are talking constantly about how the students don't seem to care or their "atrocious" behavior. The data show student achievement is not increasing the way it should, and teachers are blaming the students. The teachers then begin blaming the parents about how the parents don't care and don't support the teachers. The blame eventually ends up on the administrators for how they don't seem to care and do not support teachers.

CASE SCENARIO FOUR

You believe your meetings have become very ineffective. You have meetings every two weeks with your department (or team), but you realize nothing really happens after the meetings. The meetings are a time to share important information or discuss data, but members are really starting to feel these meetings are a waste of time. Too many talk for the sake of talking or repeat things they already said. And before you know it, the meeting time is up with nothing accomplished.

CASE SCENARIO FIVE

The school administrators just announced they are looking to change the intervention period to make it more fluid. This will allow students to go in and out of the intervention period as needed, instead of students being in the intervention period for long periods of time. In theory, you agree with this. However, in practice, you are concerned with how to take attendance, and how teachers will tell students where to go. You don't want to seem like you disagree with your administrators, but you have concerns and want to voice them.

Ask teacher leaders to anonymously submit a current scenario that describes a situation or concept they want to communicate about but maybe don't know how or where to start.

The Agree-or-Disagree Line

Invite participants to examine each of the following statements. Allow participants a few minutes to process, and then ask them to stand on the right side of the room if they agree with the statement or the left side of the room if they disagree with the statement. Once participants have chosen their side of the room, open the floor up for discussion by asking, "Why do you agree or disagree with the statement?" The discussion will help participants learn more about the importance of a teacher leader having communication skills.

> » **Statement one:** Emotions have a lot to do with how or why people miscommunicate.

> » **Statement two:** As a leader, I do not reflect on my ability to communicate well because I assume I do.

> » **Statement three:** Nonverbal communication (like body language) is just as important as verbal and written communication.

> » **Statement four:** Written communication is easier than verbal communication.

> » **Statement five:** As a teacher leader, when an interaction with a team member does not go well, I reflect on my communication.

> » **Statement six:** Communication is the most important skill to be an effective leader.

> » **Statement seven:** Communication is always the root cause of problems in my department or team.

Activity for Developing Communication Skills

The following activity provides an opportunity to practice thinking about how leaders communicate their messages. You can adapt this activity to written communication by providing scenarios that involve written communication.

Figure 13.4 is a communication activity teacher leaders can use to practice the guidance in this chapter.

1. Identify a topic you want to communicate about. Some examples to help you get started include the following.

   • Talking to a teacher in your department or team about their negative attitude

   • Telling a teacher her grading practices need to align to the team's grading practices

   • Talking to your teachers about revising their intervention block

   • Talking to teachers about organizing and presenting classroom data in a different way

   • Talking to teachers about changing some of their previous assessments to better align to standards

2. Once you select the topic, think about how you would communicate it. What would you say during a conversation to communicate your message? Write a script here.

3. Divide participants into pairs and instruct them to revise their message using the following suggestions.

   • Is your message positive?

     Eliminate any negative language in your message. Instead of what not to do, focus on what you want the recipient to do.

   • Is your message concise?

     Ensure your message is succinct. The more convoluted your message, the more confusing it is for the recipient. Stick to the request or point you want to make instead of bringing other things in or going off on a tangent.

   • Is your message specific?

     Are you giving specific directions or instructions or making a specific request so teachers have a clear understanding of your desired outcome?

   • Does your message offer help?

     How do you offer to help your teachers with the request you are making or with the directions you are giving? Do you give examples of the support they will receive or how you will help them?

   • Does your message show empathy?

     How are you connecting with the recipient to show empathy with your message? The message might be difficult for the recipient to hear, so how do you show empathy and maintain connection while communicating your request?

   • How else can you improve your message?

   • What other things can you change about your message to make it effective?

4. Have participants rewrite their message here.

5. Reflect on the differences between the first and second drafts of your message.

   • What changes did you make to your original message?

   • How or why will recipients better receive your revised message?

   • How can you apply what you learned to future communications?

FIGURE 13.4: Teacher leader communication activity.

*Visit **go.SolutionTree.com/PLCbooks** for a free reproducible of this figure.*

Summary

Communication is an essential skill leaders must have to lead effectively. Successful leadership depends on successful communication. It's not just about having effective communication skills but also constantly developing your communication skills by reflecting on how you communicate in a variety of situations. Therefore, investing time in your teacher leaders to help them develop their communication skills will help build their ability to lead. Consider how your school leadership team can use the activities in this chapter to plan your professional learning about developing communication skills.

Reflect on Developing Communication Skills

Pause to reflect on what you've read in this chapter. Use the following prompts to journal about what you learned and next steps you'll take.

Before reading this chapter, how would you have described the relationship between leadership and communication?

After reading this chapter and participating in the activities, what have you learned about your (or your teacher leaders') communication skills?

What do you plan to do to continuously strengthen your (or your teacher leaders') communication skills?

■ EPILOGUE

There is no question: strong school leadership is crucial for schools to be successful. Research shows the correlation between strong school leadership and student success (Leithwood, Louis, Anderson, & Wahlstrom, 2004; Marzano, Waters, & McNulty, 2005; Robinson, Lloyd, & Rowe, 2008). Educators know the impact school leadership has on student achievement. However, they must be clear on who defines *school leadership*. It is no longer just the principal. *School leadership* includes the principal, assistant principals, *and* teacher leaders. As a collective school leadership team, this group of school leaders is charged with improving student achievement.

Of course, ultimately everything falls to the principal. That's the purpose of this book: to help school principals build the leadership capacity of their entire school leadership team. Leaders are taught, coached, and mentored, and the school principal is responsible for providing that high quality of teaching, coaching, and mentoring to their teacher leaders. School principals can't assume that just because they made someone a teacher leader, the person knows how to lead colleagues. The school principal must develop and cultivate those leadership skills. My hope is this book equips you for that work.

Educators also know implementing a PLC is an effective way to increase student achievement. Richard DuFour and colleagues (2016) explain it this way:

> There has never been greater consensus on the most promising strategy to improve our schools. Researchers from around the world have

cited the collaborative culture, collective responsibility, transparency of practice, and unrelenting focus on each student's learning that are central to the PLC process as vital to transforming our schools. (p. 257)

But the journey to becoming a PLC requires principals to effectively lead their teams, departments, and school. I selected each of the ten key leadership skills I identify in this book because they can make a significant impact on a teacher leader's ability to effectively lead a PLC. District and school leaders should use this book with teacher leaders to create a professional development learning plan to strengthen the leadership abilities of every teacher leader in the district and school. Stronger teacher leaders can actively co-lead the PLC work with their school administrators, which ultimately leads to increased student achievement.

REFERENCES AND RESOURCES

Ackerman, C. E. (2019, February 4). *13 emotional intelligence activities, exercises & PDFs*. Accessed at https://positivepsychology.com/emotional-intelligence -exercises on October 16, 2023.

Alvoid, L., & Black, W. L., Jr. (2014). *The changing role of the principal: How high-achieving districts are recalibrating school leadership*. Washington, DC: Center for American Progress.

Amaresan, S. (2023, June 28). *27 conflict resolution skills to use with your team and your customers* [Blog post]. Accessed at https://blog.hubspot.com/service /conflict-resolution-skills on October 16, 2023.

American Society for Quality (ASQ). (n.d.). *What is a Pareto chart?* Accessed at https://asq.org/quality-resources/pareto on February 14, 2024.

Andreev, I. (2023, April 18). *Conflict management styles*. Accessed at www.valamis .com/hub/conflict-management-styles on October 16, 2023.

Axe, J. (2023, May 17). *What is problem-solving? How to use problem-solving skills to resolve issues*. Accessed at https://leaders.com/articles/productivity/problem -solving on October 16, 2023.

Axelrod, R. H. (2017). Leadership and self-confidence. In J. Marques & S. D. Dhiman (Eds.), *Leadership today: Practices for personal and professional performance* (pp. 297–314). New York: Springer.

Baker, S. J. (2022, February 25). *8 steps to be an innovative leader.* Accessed at https://theleadershipreformation.com/8-steps-to-be-an-innovative-leader on October 16, 2023.

Barnhill, A. (2023, July 21). *Effective communication: How leaders can inspire, engage and succeed.* Accessed at www.forbes.com/sites/forbescoachescouncil /2023/07/21/effective-communication-how-leaders-can-inspire-engage-and -succeed/?sh=1682abcf5023 on February 14, 2024.

Bosworth, P. (n.d.). *The power of good communication in the workplace.* Accessed at https://leadershipchoice.com/power-good-communication-workplace on October 16, 2023.

Boyd-Dimock, V., & McGree, K. M. (n.d.). *Leading change from the classroom: Teachers as leaders.* Accessed at https://sedl.org/change/issues/issues44.html on October 16, 2023.

Brearley, B. (2019, August). *Why building team confidence should be a leadership priority.* Accessed at www.thoughtfulleader.com/team-confidence on October 16, 2023.

Brown, B., & Ringwood, D. (2021, July). *Shared leadership: Creating the conditions to make it really work.* Accessed at www.mrg.com/wp-content/uploads/2021/10 /Shared-Leadership-Creating-the-Conditions-to-Make-it-Really-Work -Coaching-Perspectives-Magazine.pdf on October 16, 2023.

Buffum, A., Mattos, M., & Malone, J. (2018). *Taking action: A handbook for RTI at Work*™. Bloomington, IN: Solution Tree Press.

Busteed, B. (2020, February 17). *The really good and really bad news on lifelong learning.* Accessed at www.forbes.com/sites/brandonbusteed/2020/02/17 /the-really-good-and-really-bad-news-on-lifelong-learning/?sh=7efccbae11f2 on October 16, 2023.

CareerBuilder. (2011, August 18). *Seventy-one percent of employers say they value emotional intelligence over IQ, according to CareerBuilder survey* [Press release]. Accessed at https://press.careerbuilder.com/2011-08-18-Seventy-One-Percent -of-Employers-Say-They-Value-Emotional-Intelligence-Over-IQ-According -to-CareerBuilder-Survey on October 16, 2023.

Chowdhury, M. R. (2019, May 2). *The science & psychology of goal-setting 101.* Accessed at https://positivepsychology.com/goal-setting-psychology on February 14, 2024.

Cote, C. (2023, January 17). *Why problem-solving skills are essential for leaders in any industry* [Blog post]. Accessed at https://online.hbs.edu/blog/post/problem -solving-in-business on February 14, 2024.

Couros, G. (2015). *The innovator's mindset: Empower learning, unleash talent, and lead a culture of creativity.* San Diego, CA: Burgess.

CPP. (2008, July). *Workplace conflict and how businesses can harness it to thrive* [Report]. Accessed at www.themyersbriggs.com/-/media/f39a8b7fb4fe4 daface552d9f485c825.ashx on October 16, 2023.

Credibility. (n.d.). In *Merriam-Webster's online dictionary.* Accessed at www.merriam -webster.com/dictionary/credibility on October 18, 2023.

DeWitt, P. (2021, May 16). *Stress, anxiety, initiative fatigue . . . Oh my! Perhaps it's time to "de-implement"?* Accessed at www.edweek.org/leadership /opinion-stress-anxiety-initiative-fatigue-oh-my-perhaps-its-time-to-de -implement/2021/05 on February 14, 2024.

Draghici, A. (2023, May 7). *11 benefits of improving your emotional intelligence* [Blog post]. Accessed at www.happierhuman.com/benefits-emotional-intelligence on October 16, 2023.

DuFour, R. (n.d.). *Effective leaders don't leave learning to chance* [Video file]. Accessed at www.solutiontree.com/globalpdteams on October 18, 2023.

DuFour, R., & DuFour, R. (2012). *The school leader's guide to Professional Learning Communities at Work.* Bloomington, IN: Solution Tree Press.

DuFour, R., DuFour, R., Eaker, R., Many, T. W., & Mattos, M. (2016). *Learning by doing: A handbook for Professional Learning Communities at Work* (3rd ed.). Bloomington, IN: Solution Tree Press.

DuFour, R., DuFour, R., Eaker, R., Many, T. W., Mattos, M., & Muhammad, A. (2024). *Learning by doing: A handbook for Professional Learning Communities at Work* (4th ed.). Bloomington, IN: Solution Tree Press.

DuFour, R., DuFour, R., Eaker, R., Mattos, M., & Muhammad, A. (2021). *Revisiting Professional Learning Communities at Work: Proven insights for sustained, substantive school improvement* (2nd ed.). Bloomington, IN: Solution Tree Press.

DuFour, R., & Eaker, R. (1998). *Professional Learning Communities at Work: Best practices for enhancing student achievement.* Bloomington, IN: Solution Tree Press.

DuFour, R., & Fullan, M. (2013). *Cultures built to last: Systemic PLCs at Work.* Bloomington, IN: Solution Tree Press.

DuFour, R., & Marzano, R. J. (2011). *Leaders of learning: How district, school, and classroom leaders improve student achievement.* Bloomington, IN: Solution Tree Press.

Eaker, R. (2020). *A summing up: Teaching & learning in effective schools & PLCs at Work.* Bloomington, IN: Solution Tree Press.

Eisler, M. (2021, August 17). *6 activities to spark creativity and innovation on your team.* Accessed at https://widelensleadership.com/6-activities-to-spark -creativity-and-innovation-on-your-team on October 17, 2023.

Emotional intelligence. (n.d.). In *Merriam-Webster's online dictionary.* Accessed at www.merriam-webster.com/dictionary/emotional%20intelligence on October 18, 2023.

Forbes Coaches Council. (2020, July 16). *13 telltale signs that a manager is micromanaging their team.* Accessed at www.forbes.com/sites/forbescoachesco uncil/2020/07/16/13-telltale-signs-that-a-manager-is-micromanaging-their -team/?sh=4a45f65e1ccb on October 17, 2023.

Fullan, M. (2014). *The principal: Three keys to maximizing impact.* San Fransisco: Jossey-Bass.

Fullan, M. (2023). *The principal 2.0: Three keys to maximizing impact* (2nd ed.). Hoboken, NJ: Wiley.

Gallo, C. (2022, November 23). *How great leaders communicate.* Accessed at https://hbr.org/2022/11/how-great-leaders-communicate on February 14, 2024.

Garramone, N. (2020, February 11). *Know, do, deal: Differentiating between healthy & unhealthy conflict.* Accessed at https://oneeighty.medium.com/4-steps-for -dealing-with-unhealthy-conflict-7ab77ece456b on October 17, 2023.

Georgia Leadership Institute for School Improvement (GLISI). (2015, October). *Cultivating teacher leadership: Where do principals begin?* [Research brief].

Accessed at https://glisi.wpenginepowered.com/wp-content/uploads/2015/11 /Teacher-Leadership_Research-Brief_Final-Updated.pdf on October 17, 2023.

Goldsmith, M. (2010, May 26). *Sharing leadership to maximize talent.* Accessed at https://hbr.org/2010/05/sharing-leadership-to-maximize on October 17, 2023.

Goleman, D. (1995). *Emotional intelligence: Why it can matter more than IQ.* New York: Bantam Books.

Goleman, D. (2020). *Emotional intelligence: Why it can matter more than IQ* (2nd ed.). London: Bloomsbury.

Goleman, D., Boyatzis, R., & McKee, A. (2013). *Primal leadership: Unleashing the power of emotional intelligence.* Boston: Harvard Business Review Press.

Gordon, K. (2021). *The three chairs: How great leaders drive communication, performance, and engagement.* Gold River, CA: Authority.

Grady, A. (2016, May 4). *7 steps for keeping conflict healthy.* Accessed at www.entrepreneur.com/leadership/7-steps-for-keeping-conflict-healthy /272298 on October 17, 2023.

Gray, K. D. (n.d.). *5 steps to good decision making.* Accessed at www.corporate wellnessmagazine.com/article/5-steps-to-good-decision-making on October 17, 2023.

Grenny, J., Patterson, K., McMillan, R., Switzler, A., & Gregory, E. (2022). *Crucial conversations: Tools for talking when stakes are high* (3rd ed.). New York: McGraw-Hill.

Hall, B. (2022). *Powerful guiding coalitions: How to build and sustain the leadership team in your PLC at Work.* Bloomington, IN: Solution Tree Press.

Harrison, C., & Killion, J. (2007). Ten roles for teacher leaders. *Educational Leadership, 65*(1), 74–77.

Hattie, J. (2023). *Visible learning: The sequel—A synthesis of over 2,100 meta-analyses relating to achievement.* London: Routledge, Taylor & Francis.

Jee, G. (2022, May 18). *Questioning for innovation.* Accessed at https://talenttalks.net /questioning-for-innovation on October 17, 2023.

Jones, R. (2015). *A new strategy to identify teacher leaders.* Accessed at www.naesp.org /sites/default/files/Jones_JF15.pdf on October 17, 2023.

Kanold, T. D., & Boogren, T. H. (2022). *Educator wellness: A guide for sustaining physical, mental, emotional, and social well-being.* Bloomington, IN: Solution Tree Press.

Keating, K. (2020, May 26). *The mindset of a lifelong learner.* Accessed at www.chieflearningofficer.com/2020/05/26/the-mindset-of-a-lifelong-learner on October 17, 2023.

Kilmann Diagnostics. (n.d.). *Thomas-Kilmann Instrument (TKI): 1 TKI per person.* Accessed at https://kilmanndiagnostics.com/assessments/thomas-kilmann -instrument-one-assessment-person on October 17, 2023.

Kirtman, L. (2014). *Leadership and teams: The missing piece of the educational reform puzzle.* Boston: Pearson.

Knight, R. (2015, January 9). *How to handle difficult conversations at work.* Accessed at https://hbr.org/2015/01/how-to-handle-difficult-conversations-at-work on October 17, 2023.

Kotter. (n.d.). *The 8 steps for leading change.* Accessed at www.kotterinc.com /methodology/8-steps on February 19, 2024.

Kotter, J. P. (2012). *Leading change.* Boston: Harvard Review Press. Accessed at https://google.com/books/edition/Leading_Change/xpGX1EWL _EMC?hl=en&gbpv=1&dq=leading+change&printsec=frontcover on February 22, 2024.

Kullar, J. K. (2020). *Connecting through leadership: The promise of precise and effective communication in schools.* Bloomington, IN: Solution Tree Press.

Laker, B., & Pereira, V. (2022, May 31). *4 triggers cause the majority of team conflicts.* Accessed at https://hbr.org/2022/05/conflict-is-not-always-bad-but-you -should-know-how-to-manage-it on October 17, 2023.

Lancefield, D., & Rangen, C. (2021, May 5). *4 actions transformational leaders take.* Accessed at https://hbr.org/2021/05/4-actions-transformational-leaders-take on October 17, 2023.

Landry, L. (2019, April 3). *Why emotional intelligence is important in leadership* [Blog post]. Accessed at https://online.hbs.edu/blog/post/emotional-intelligence-in -leadership on October 17, 2023.

Latham, A. (2021a, July 20). *Clarity is important, but are you clear enough?* Accessed at www.forbes.com/sites/annlatham/2021/07/20/clarity-is-important-but-we-are -clear-enough-right/?sh=344c4218615e on October 17, 2023.

Latham, A. (2021b). *The power of clarity: Unleash the true potential of workplace productivity, confidence, and empowerment.* London: Bloomsbury Business.

Leading Across London. (2014). *Emotional intelligence questionnaire: Outcomes measurement tool.* London: NHS England. Accessed at www.drugsandalcohol .ie/26776/1/Emotional_intelligence_questionnaire-LAL1.pdf.

Leithwood, K., Louis, K. S., Anderson, S., & Wahlstrom, K. (2004). *How leadership influences student learning* [Research review]. New York: The Wallace Foundation. Accessed at www.wallacefoundation.org/knowledge -center/documents/how-leadership-influences-student-learning.pdf on October 17, 2023.

Livingston, C. (1992). Introduction: Teacher leadership for restructured schools. In C. Livingston (Ed.), *Teachers as leaders: Evolving roles* (pp. 9–17). Washington, DC: National Education Association.

Llopis, G. (2013, November 4). *The 4 most effective ways leaders solve problems.* Accessed at https://forbes.com/sites/glennllopis/2013/11/04/the-4 -most-effective-ways-leaders-solve-problems/?sh=4c94f7d54f97 on February 15, 2024.

Lynch, M. (2023, March 30). *There have been 376 school shootings since Columbine.* Accessed at www.theedadvocate.org/there-have-been-376-school-shootings -since-columbine on October 17, 2023.

Marzano, R. J., Waters, T., & McNulty, B. A. (2005). *School leadership that works: From research to results.* Alexandria, VA: ASCD.

Mattos, M., Buffum, A., Malone, J., Cruz, L. F., Dimich, N., & Schuhl, S. (in press). *Taking action: A handbook for RTI at Work* (2nd ed.). Bloomington, IN: Solution Tree Press.

Maxfield, B. (2019, October 3). *Office haunting: 8 out of 10 employees are running in fear from a scary conversation at work.* Accessed at https://cruciallearning.com /press/employees-run-from-uncomfortable-conversations-crucial-learning on October 17, 2023.

McGroarty, K. (2022, March 8). *4 creative conflict resolution activities for workplace* [Blog post]. Accessed at https://pollackpeacebuilding.com/blog/4-conflict -resolution-activities-for-workplace on October 17, 2023.

Mind Tools Content Team. (n.d.). *5 Whys*. Accessed at https://mindtools.com /a3mi00v/5-whys on March 5, 2024.

Moore, C. (2019, May 21). *15 communication exercises and games for the workplace.* Accessed at https://positivepsychology.com/communication-exercises-for-work on October 17, 2023.

Muha, T. (2016, June 12). *Achieving happiness: Confidence is essential to teamwork.* Accessed at www.capitalgazette.com/lifestyles/ph-ac-muha-0612-20160612 -story.html on October 17, 2023.

National Education Association. (2018). *The teacher leadership competencies.* Accessed at https://nea.org/sites/default/files/2021-03/2019%20TLI%20 Competency%20Book%20NEA_TLCF_20180824.pdf on October 16, 2018.

New Leaders. (2015a). *Untapped: A policy roadmap for improving schools through shared leadership, version 2.0.* New York: Author. Accessed at https://assets-global .website-files.com/61b0e0e7cf389b116afdcabf/620c204a33e8090789705149 _Untapped_PolicyRoadmap%20%26%20Case%20Study.pdf on October 17, 2023.

New Leaders. (2015b). *Untapped: Transforming teacher leadership to help students succeed* [Executive summary]. New York: Author. Accessed at https://files.eric .ed.gov/fulltext/ED584851.pdf on October 17, 2023.

Nichols, R. (n.d.). *What is lifelong learning, and why should you turn employees into lifelong learners?* Accessed at https://360learning.com/guide/learning-theories /lifelong-learning on October 17, 2023.

Nicola. (2023, September 9). *Thirteen reasons why it's so hard to make a decision.* Accessed at https://wisdomstirring.com/article/why-its-so-hard-to-make-a -decision on February 20, 2024.

Nordstrom, N. M., & Merz, J. F. (2006). *Learning later, living greater: The secret for making the most of your after-50 years.* Boulder, CO: Sentient.

Organizational Psychology Degrees. (n.d.). *What is collective intelligence?* Accessed at www.organizationalpsychologydegrees.com/faq/what-is-collective-intelligence on November 10, 2023.

Reeves, D. (2021). *Deep change leadership: A model for renewing and strengthening schools and districts.* Bloomington, IN: Solution Tree Press.

Reid, D. C. (2022, September 7). *Coaching leaders from insecure to secure* [Blog post]. Accessed at www.psychologytoday.com/us/blog/coaching-corner/202209 /coaching-leaders-insecure-secure on October 17, 2023.

Robinson, V. M. J., Lloyd, C. A., & Rowe, K. J. (2008). The impact of leadership on student outcomes: An analysis of the differential effects of leadership types. *Educational Administration Quarterly, 44*(5), 635–674.

Salovey, P., & Mayer, J. D. (1990). Emotional intelligence. *Imagination, Cognition and Personality, 9*(3), 185–211.

Sanfilippo, M. (2023, February 21). *Shared leadership: How modern businesses run themselves.* Accessed at www.businessnewsdaily.com/135-shared-leadership -social-media-fuel-business-growth.html on October 17, 2023.

Sharma, S. (2023, August 10). *How healthy conflict in the workplace boosts productivity: 5 benefits.* Accessed at www.risely.me/5-benefits-of-healthy-conflict-at-work on October 17, 2023.

Shen, J., Wu, H., Reeves, P., Zheng, Y., Ryan, L., & Anderson, D. (2020). The association between teacher leadership and student achievement: A meta-analysis. *Educational Research Review, 31.* https://doi.org/10.1016/j .edurev.2020.100357

Skills Converged. (2017, August 21). *Emotional intelligence exercise: Temperament analysis* [Blog post]. Accessed at www.skillsconverged.com/blogs/free-training-materials/emotional-intelligence-exercise-temperament-analysis on October 17, 2023.

Spiller, J., & Power, K. (2022). *Leading beyond intention: 6 areas to deepen reflection and planning in your PLC at Work.* Bloomington, IN: Solution Tree Press.

SYDLE. (2023, May 18). *Lifelong learning: Why is it important for people and institutions?* [Blog post]. Accessed at www.sydle.com/blog/lifelong-learning -61f94590eca9c55ca5c4ea6a on October 18, 2023.

Teacher Leadership Exploratory Consortium. (n.d.). *Teacher leader model standards.* Accessed at www.ets.org/content/dam/ets-org/pdfs/patl/patl-teacher-leader -model-standards.pdf on October 18, 2023.

Teacher-Led Professional Learning. (n.d.). *Selecting teacher-leaders.* Accessed at www.teacherledprofessionallearning.org/steps/selecting-teacher-leaders on October 17, 2023.

Temperament. (2023, October 27). In *Britannica's online dictionary.* Accessed at www.britannica.com/topic/temperament on January 5, 2024.

Trotta, J. (2022, May 25). *Courageous leadership and why it matters.* Accessed at www.linkedin.com/pulse/courageous-leadership-why-matters-joanne -trotta-she-her-?trk=pulse-article_more-articles_related-content-card on October 18, 2023.

Tucker, R. (2017, February 9). *Six innovation leadership skills everybody needs to master.* Accessed at https://forbes.com/sites/robertbtucker/2017/02/09/six-innovation -leadership-skills-everybody-needs-to-master/?sh=56ec696a5d46 on February 9, 2017.

Wendland, D. (2023, January 13). *Brainstorming more effectively.* Accessed at www.forbes.com/sites/forbesagencycouncil/2023/01/13/brainstorming-more -effectively/?sh=4db34fe53252 on October 18, 2023.

Wenning, M. (2017, January 2). *Why failure is so important for a successful innovation strategy* [Blog post]. Accessed at www.hypeinnovation.com/blog/why-failure -is-an-essential-component-of-a-strong-innovation-strategy on October 18, 2023.

Whitener, S. (2022, December 30). *Why is emotional intelligence important?* Accessed at www.forbes.com/sites/forbescoachescouncil/2022/12/30/why-is-emotional -intelligence-important/?sh=18df4d8c3289 on October 18, 2023.

Wilding, M. (2020, July 27). *How to be a confident, concise communicator (even when you have to speak off the cuff).* Accessed at www.forbes.com/sites/melody wilding/2020/07/27/how-to-be-a-confident-concise-communicator-even -when-you-have-to-speak-off-the-cuff/?sh=7355a1101fe1 on October 18, 2023.

Wilhelm, T. (2013, October 1). *How principals cultivate shared leadership.* Accessed at www.ascd.org/el/articles/how-principals-cultivate-shared-leadership on October 18, 2023.

Wilhelm, T. (2017, August 31). *The benefits and drawbacks of shared leadership.* Accessed at https://corwin-connect.com/2017/08/benefits-drawbacks-shared -leadership on October 18, 2023.

Williams, K. C., & Hierck, T. (2015). *Starting a movement: Building culture from the inside out in professional learning communities.* Bloomington, IN: Solution Tree Press.

Wilson, M. (1993). The search for teacher leaders. *Educational Leadership, 50*(6), 24–27.

Wiseman, L. (2017). *Multipliers: How the best leaders make everyone smarter.* New York: HarperBusiness.

Yilmaz, E. (2023). *Temperaments: Definitions, examples and types.* Accessed at www.berkeleywellbeing.com/temperaments.html on February 15, 2024.

Zinn, L. F. (1997, March). *Supports and barriers to teacher leadership: Reports of teacher leaders.* Paper presented at the annual meeting of the American Educational Research Association, Chicago. Accessed at https://files.eric.ed.gov/fulltext/ED408259.pdf on October 18, 2023.

■ INDEX

Teacher Leaders, Classroom Champions

Jeanetta Jones Miller

Gain a clear path to activate school improvement from within your classroom. This book shares a vision of teacher leadership not as teachers who lead other teachers but as those who take responsibility in supporting other teachers, students, and parents in a variety of ways.

BKG110

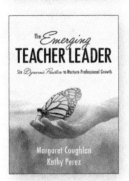

The Emerging Teacher Leader

Margaret Coughlan and Kathy Perez

Packed with insights from veteran teacher leaders, this book equips educators with six dynamic practices to empower their expertise and inspire their peers. Discover how to amplify success in the classroom and become agents for change and school improvement.

BKG057

Connecting Through Leadership

Jasmine K. Kullar

The success of a school greatly depends on the ability of its leaders to communicate effectively. Rely on *Connecting Through Leadership* to help you strengthen your communication skills to inspire, motivate, and connect with every member of your school community.

BKF927

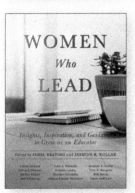

Women Who Lead

Edited by Janel Keating and Jasmine K. Kullar

Get motivated by this collection of voices from women in educational leadership and their allies. This book offers insight and guidance on effective leadership practices, how to navigate roadblocks and complications specific to women, and how to nurture your own professional growth.

BKF991

Solution Tree | Press

a division of

Solution Tree

Visit SolutionTree.com or call 800.733.6786 to order.

Global PD teams
Collaborative Learning for School Improvement

Quality team learning **from authors you trust**

Global PD Teams is the first-ever **online professional development resource designed to support your entire faculty on your learning journey.** This convenient tool offers daily access to videos, mini-courses, eBooks, articles, and more packed with insights and research-backed strategies you can use immediately.

GET STARTED
SolutionTree.com/**GlobalPDTeams**
800.733.6786

Solution Tree